Review,
Practice,
& Mastery of

Common Core

Mathematics

State Standards

Reviewers

Deanna Avery • Nantucket Public Schools • Nantucket, MA
Melinda Baer • Saddleback Valley Unified School District • Lake Forest, CA
Theresa Casto • Northern Wells Community Schools • Bluffton, IN
Michelle Cox • Southwestern Community School District • Piasa, IL
Christine Dolan • Marlborough Public Schools • Marlborough, MA
Rebecca Haas • Illinois Public School District • Aurora, IL
Angela Kulacz • Elmhurst Unit School District • Elmhurst, IL
Suzan A. Lambert • Rowan-Salisbury School District • Salisbury, NC
Louise Leon • Florence Township Schools • Florence, NJ
Pamela Lucchesi • Region 12 • Roxbury, CT
Aaron Moring-D'Angier • Cook County Schools • Chicago, IL
Bruce Rainwater • San Diego Unified • San Diego, CA
Shantell Toups • St. Mary Parish • Berwick, LA
Debbie Smith • Opp City Schools • Opp, AL
Cheryl Wild • Higley Unified School District • Gilbert, AZ

© 2015 by Perfection Learning®

Please visit our Web site at
www.perfectionlearning.com

When ordering this book, please specify:
ISBN 978-0-7891-8941-7 or **94188**

3 4 5 6 7 PP 19 18 17 16 15

Printed in the United States of America

To the Student

This book will help you review, practice, and master the Common Core State Standards for Mathematics. Here are the steps to follow to use this book.

1. Take the Tryout Test and check your answers. Use the chart at the bottom of this page to find out your strengths and weaknesses in the areas covered. Don't be discouraged if you don't get all the answers right or if you don't understand some questions. Remember the questions that are hard for you to answer. They will be the types of questions you need to work on the most.

2. Work through the lessons that follow the Tryout Test. Each lesson reviews example items and provides a practice test based on the Common Core State Standards. Fill in the Keeping Score chart on page 103 as you complete each practice test.

3. After completing all the lessons, take the Mastery Test. Your score on this test will show your understanding of the Common Core State Standards for Mathematics.

Unit	Tryout Test Items	Mastery Test Items
1 Algebraic Thinking	1, 2, 3, 4, 5, 6	1, 2, 3, 4, 5, 6
2 Number Sense	7, 8, 9, 10, 11, 12, 13, 14, 15, 16, 17, 18	7, 8, 9, 10, 11, 12, 13, 14, 15, 16, 17, 18
3 Operations with Whole Numbers and Decimals	19, 20, 21, 22, 23, 24, 25, 26	19, 20, 21, 22, 23, 24, 25, 26
4 Fractions	27, 28, 29, 30, 31, 32, 33, 34, 35, 36, 37	27, 28, 29, 30, 31, 32, 33, 34, 35, 36, 37
5 Measurement and Data	38, 39, 40, 41, 42, 43, 44, 45	38, 39, 40, 41, 42, 43, 44, 45
6 Geometry	46, 47, 48, 49, 50	46, 47, 48, 49, 50

Common Core
Math
5

Table of Contents

Table of Contents *continued*

Tryout Test

Estimated time: 60 minutes

Directions: Read each question and choose the best answer.

1 Evaluate this expression.

$$[(25 - 14) \times 2 - 12] \div 2$$

Ⓐ 3

Ⓑ 5

Ⓒ 11

Ⓓ 16

2 Which expression shows a number 4 times greater than 796 + 812?

Ⓐ 4 × (796 + 812)

Ⓑ (796 + 812) ÷ 4

Ⓒ (4 × 796) + 812

Ⓓ (796 + 812) + 4

3 Marcie subtracted 17 from 58 and then multiplied by the sum of 6 and 8. Write the expression she used.

Answer: _____

4 Which expression can Will evaluate to find the distance to the grocery store and back if he walks 8 blocks east and 3 blocks south to get to the grocery store?

Ⓐ 2 + 8 + 3

Ⓑ 2 × 8 + 3

Ⓒ (8 + 3) × 2

Ⓓ (8 × 2) × (3 × 2)

5 What is the value of the expression?

$$3 + \{6 + [10 - 3 \times (2 + 1)] + 1\}$$

Answer: _____

6 Start at zero and write a sequence for each of these rules:

    Add 4

    Add 8

Describe the relationship between the corresponding terms in the two sequences.

Add 4: 0, _____

Add 8: 0, _____

_____

7 In the number 22,222, how many times greater is the 2 in the thousands place than the 2 in the hundreds place?

Ⓐ 1 time

Ⓑ 9 times

Ⓒ 10 times

Ⓓ 100 times

8 Which describes how to move the decimal point to multiply by 0.01?

Ⓐ Move the decimal point 1 place to the right.

Ⓑ Move the decimal point 1 place to the left.

Ⓒ Move the decimal point 2 places to the right.

Ⓓ Move the decimal point 2 places to the left.

GO ON

5

9 How much will 1,000 pens cost if 1 pen costs $1.19?

Answer: _____

10 Ben bought 100 tulip bulbs for $53.60. What was the cost of each bulb?

Answer: _____

11 Write 10,000 in exponential notation.

Answer: _____

12 Write 10^1 in standard form.

Answer: _____

13 What is the standard form for
$600,000 + 40,000 + 200 + 70 + 0.9 + 0.05$?

- Ⓐ 640,270.95
- Ⓒ 64,270.95
- Ⓑ 604,207.095
- Ⓓ 642,270,095

14 What is the place value of 4 in the number 5,236.147?

- Ⓐ hundreds
- Ⓒ hundredths
- Ⓑ tenths
- Ⓓ thousandths

15 Write 56.437 in word form.

Answer: _____

16 Which answer choice shows *two hundred twenty-seven and four hundredths*?

- Ⓐ 0.02274
- Ⓒ 227.04
- Ⓑ 227.004
- Ⓓ 227.4

17 Write >, =, or < to compare these decimals.

29.052 ☐ 29.502

Answer: _____

18 Adam bought 3.158 pounds of salmon. To the nearest tenth of a pound, how much salmon did he buy?

- Ⓐ 3.16 lb
- Ⓒ 3.1 lb
- Ⓑ 3.2 lb
- Ⓓ 3 lb

19 $623 \times 71 =$

- Ⓐ 4,984
- Ⓒ 44,233
- Ⓑ 5,084
- Ⓓ 44,242

20 What number goes in the box in the number sentence below?

$$8 \times \square = 56$$

Answer: _____

21 There are 868 seats in a theater arranged in 28 equal rows. How many seats are in each row?

- Ⓐ 31
- Ⓒ 43
- Ⓑ 41
- Ⓓ 46

22 Annamaria paid $13.14 for 6 notebooks. What was the cost of each notebook?

- Ⓐ $2.19
- Ⓒ $21.90
- Ⓑ $2.79
- Ⓓ $78.84

23 Oranges cost $1.29 a pound. How much will 3.6 pounds of oranges cost? Round up to the nearest cent. Show your work below.

Answer: _____

24 The table shows prices of items at a clothing store.

Item	Price
T-shirt	$9.95
Shorts	$15.25
Pants	$18.75
Sunglasses	$1.95
Flip-flops	$9.59
Baseball hat	$8.50

Jamie bought 2 pairs of flip-flops. She gave the clerk a $20 bill. How much change should she receive?

Ⓐ $0.18   Ⓒ $1.82
Ⓑ $0.82   Ⓓ $1.92

25 George shipped two boxes weighing 0.9 pounds and 5.25 pounds. What was the total weight of the two boxes?

Ⓐ 5.15 pounds   Ⓒ 5.34 pounds
Ⓑ 5.24 pounds   Ⓓ 6.15 pounds

26 Miguel needs 1.2 liters of milk for a recipe. He has 0.5 liters. How much more does he need?

Ⓐ 6.2 L   Ⓒ 1.7 L
Ⓑ 1.9 L   Ⓓ 0.7 L

27 A deli sandwich has $\frac{1}{8}$ pound of sliced turkey and $\frac{1}{4}$ pound of sliced American cheese. What is the total weight of the turkey and cheese?

Ⓐ $\frac{1}{8}$ pound   Ⓒ $\frac{3}{8}$ pound
Ⓑ $\frac{1}{4}$ pound   Ⓓ $\frac{1}{2}$ pound

28 Alicia measured her bean plant and announced it was $\frac{1}{3}$ foot tall. Her friend Marcia said her bean plant was $\frac{1}{4}$ foot tall. How much taller was Alicia's plant?

Ⓐ $\frac{1}{12}$ ft   Ⓒ $\frac{1}{7}$ ft
Ⓑ $\frac{7}{12}$ ft   Ⓓ $\frac{2}{7}$ ft

29 It took George $14\frac{1}{4}$ hours to plant a vegetable garden. Dirk planted his garden in $9\frac{3}{4}$ hours. How much longer did it take George to plant his garden than Dirk?

Ⓐ $3\frac{1}{4}$ hours   Ⓒ $4\frac{1}{4}$ hours
Ⓑ $3\frac{1}{2}$ hours   Ⓓ $4\frac{1}{2}$ hours

30 If 6 people divide 5 pounds of nuts evenly, how many pounds of nuts will each person get?

Ⓐ $\frac{5}{6}$ lb
Ⓑ $1\frac{1}{5}$ lb
Ⓒ 11 lb
Ⓓ 30 lb

31 If Amy pours a 32-ounce bottle of juice equally into 5 glasses, about how many ounces of juice will be in each glass? Show your work below.

Ⓐ between 4 ounces and 5 ounces
Ⓑ between 5 ounces and 6 ounces
Ⓒ between 6 ounces and 7 ounces
Ⓓ between 7 ounces and 8 ounces

32 Andrew needs to find $\frac{1}{5}$ of 65. Which expression can he use?

Ⓐ $\frac{1}{65} \times 5$

Ⓑ $65 \div 5$

Ⓒ 65×5

Ⓓ $\frac{1}{65} \div 5$

33 Use this area model to help you find the product $\frac{1}{5} \times \frac{3}{4}$.

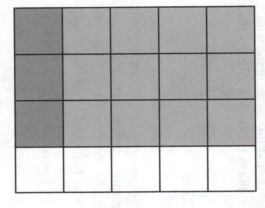

Answer: _____

34 Which statement describes the product of $4\frac{2}{3} \times \frac{3}{5}$?

Ⓐ The product is less than $4\frac{2}{3}$.

Ⓑ The product is greater than $4\frac{2}{3}$.

Ⓒ The product is less than $\frac{3}{5}$.

Ⓓ The product is 1.

35 Greg rode his bicycle at $8\frac{1}{2}$ miles per hour for $1\frac{1}{2}$ hours. How far did he ride?

Ⓐ 7 miles

Ⓑ 10 miles

Ⓒ $10\frac{1}{4}$ miles

Ⓓ $12\frac{3}{4}$ miles

36 Asaad had $\frac{1}{2}$ of a sheet of wrapping paper. He divided it into 5 equal pieces. What fraction of the sheet of wrapping paper was each piece?

Answer: _____

37 How many $\frac{1}{4}$-pound bags of raisins can Dara make from 4 pounds of raisins?

Answer: _____

38 How many inches are in 24 feet?

Answer: _____

39 Which measure is equal to 850 grams?

Ⓐ 0.85 kg   Ⓒ 85 kg

Ⓑ 8.5 kg   Ⓓ 8,500 kg

40 How can you change feet into yards?

Ⓐ Divide by 3.

Ⓑ Multiply by 3.

Ⓒ Multiply by 12.

Ⓓ Divide by 12.

41 Jake needs 180 inches of a wallpaper border to put around a window. He has $3\frac{1}{2}$ yards. How many more inches of the border does he need? Show your work below.

Answer: _____

42 Zahra measured the widths of some pictures she cut out of magazines and made this line plot of the data.

Picture Widths

	X			X
	X	X		X
X	X	X		X
X	X	X	X	X
X	X	X	X	X
$2\frac{1}{8}$	$2\frac{1}{4}$	$2\frac{3}{8}$		$2\frac{1}{2}$

Width (in inches)

If she arranges all of the pictures that are more than $2\frac{1}{4}$ inches wide side by side in a row, how long will the row of pictures be?

Answer: _____

43 What is the volume of this rectangular prism?

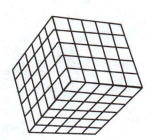

Ⓐ 70 cubic units

Ⓑ 85 cubic units

Ⓒ 120 cubic units

Ⓓ 150 cubic units

44 How many cubic yards of dirt must be removed to make a hole that is 10 yards deep, 12 yards long, and 5 yards wide?

Ⓐ 27 yd^3 Ⓒ 600 yd^3

Ⓑ 270 yd^3 Ⓓ 6,000 yd^3

45 Russ rents two storage lockers. One is 12 feet long, 10 feet wide, and 8 feet tall. The other is 10 feet long, 6 feet wide, and 8 feet tall. What is the total volume of the two lockers?

Show all of your work. Explain in words the steps you followed. Write your answer on the answer line.

Answer: _____

Explanation: _____

_____

_____

Marcus made this drawing to show where he is putting the nails to hold pictures on his wall. Use this coordinate grid for questions 46 and 47.

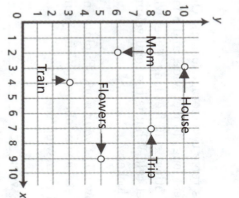

46 What picture is he putting at point (7, 8)?

Ⓐ Flowers

Ⓑ House

Ⓒ Mom

Ⓓ Trip

47 What ordered pair shows the location of the train picture?

Ⓐ (3, 4)

Ⓑ (4, 3)

Ⓒ (4, 4)

Ⓓ (3, 3)

48 Start at 20. Write sequences for the rules *Subtract 4* and *Subtract 2*. Use corresponding terms from the patterns to make ordered pairs. Graph the ordered pairs on the coordinate grid at the top of the next column.

Subtract 4: 20, _____

Subtract 2: 20, _____

Describe the pattern shown by the points.

Answer: _____

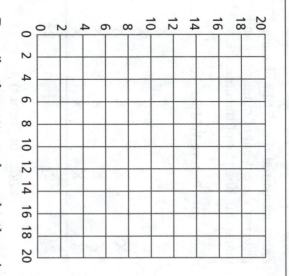

49 Which statement is true?

Ⓐ All squares are rectangles.

Ⓑ All trapezoids are parallelograms.

Ⓒ All trapezoids are triangles.

Ⓓ A rectangle has acute angles.

50 Classify this quadrilateral.

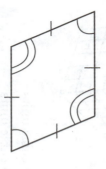

Ⓐ trapezoid, parallelogram, rectangle

Ⓑ quadrilateral, parallelogram, rhombus

Ⓒ parallelogram, rectangle, rhombus

Ⓓ parallelogram, rhombus, square

STOP

Points Earned/Total = _____ /50

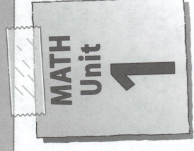

MATH Unit 1

Algebraic Thinking

1 Evaluating Expressions **[5.OA.1]**
2 Writing Expressions **[5.OA.2]**
3 Interpreting Expressions **[5.OA.2]**
4 Analyzing Patterns and Relationships **[5.OA.3]**
  Unit 1 Application **[5.OA.1, 5.OA.2]**

Directions: Answer each question.

Evaluating Expressions

1 Evaluate this expression.

   $[5 + (9 - 3)] \times 2$

Answer: _____

Grouping Symbols

Groupings of symbols tell you the order in which to do operations. Parentheses ( ), brackets [ ], and braces { } are common grouping symbols. This expression uses all three types of symbols.

   $3\{4 + [2 (6 - 5)] + 8\}$

Notice that parentheses are the innermost symbols, then brackets, then braces { [( )] }. Evaluate from the inside out. Start with parentheses, then brackets, and then braces.

Step-By-Step

For **example 1**, evaluate within parentheses first.

1 Evaluate $(9 - 3)$.

   $[5 + (9 - 3)] \times 2 =$

   $[5 + \boxed{}] \times 2$

2 Evaluate within brackets.

   $[5 + 6] \times 2 =$

   $\boxed{} \times 2$

3 Multiply.

   $11 \times 2 = \boxed{}$

GO ON →

2 Evaluate this expression.

$$\{4 + [8 \div 4 \times (3 - 1)] \times 3\} + 1$$

Answer: _____

Order of Operations

1 Do operations within grouping symbols.

2 Evaluate exponents.

3 Multiply and divide from left to right.

4 Add and subtract from left to right.

Step-By-Step

Use the **order of operations** to evaluate the expression for **example 2**.

1 Evaluate within parentheses first.

$$\{4 + [8 \div 4 \times (3 - 1)] \times 3\} + 1 =$$

$$\{4 + [8 \div 4 \times \boxed{}] \times 3\} + 1$$

2 Evaluate within brackets. Multiply and divide from left to right.

$$\{4 + [8 \div 4 \times 2] \times 3\} + 1 =$$

$$\{4 + \boxed{} \times 3\} + 1$$

3 Evaluate within braces. Multiply first, then add.

$$\{4 + 4 \times 3\} + 1 =$$

$$\boxed{} + 1$$

4 Add.

$$16 + 1 = \boxed{}$$

Writing Expressions

3 To find the number of seconds in $4\frac{1}{2}$ minutes, Gabe multiplied 4 times 60 and added 30. Which expression did he use?

Ⓐ $4 \times 30 + 60$

Ⓑ $4 \times 60 + 30$

Ⓒ $4 \times 60 + 4 \times 30$

Ⓓ $4 + (60 + 30)$

Step-By-Step

For **example 3**, write the verbal expression as a numerical expression.

1 Write *4 times 60* numerically.

$$4 \qquad \boxed{} \qquad 60$$

2 Write *add 30* numerically.

$$4 \times 60 + \boxed{}$$

Writing Expressions

4 Mary is 3 years more than twice as old as Dan. If Dan is d years old, how old is Mary?

  Ⓐ $2d - 3$ Ⓒ $3d - 2$

  Ⓑ $2d + 3$ Ⓓ $3d + 2$

Step-By-Step

For **example 4**, you need to write an expression to represent Mary's age. Use the words in the problem to determine the correct expression.

1 *Mary is three years more . . .*

$$+ 3$$

2 *. . . than twice as old as Dan.*

$$2 \times d \text{ or } 2d$$

3 Put the two parts of the expression together.

Interpreting Expressions

Chipper Rental
$42 per hour
Delivery fee $30

5 What question can be answered by evaluating this expression?

$$(6 \times 42) + 30$$

  Ⓐ How much does it cost to rent 6 chippers?

  Ⓑ What is the cost to rent the chipper for 30 hours?

  Ⓒ How much does it cost to rent a chipper for 6 hours?

  Ⓓ How much more is the chipper rental than the delivery fee?

6 The perimeter of a rectangle is calculated using this expression.

$$2 \times (45 + 60)$$

Which expression can be used to find the amount of ribbon needed to go around the perimeter of the rectangle 4 times?

  Ⓐ $4 \times [2 \times (45 + 60)]$

  Ⓑ $4 + [2 \times (45 + 60)]$

  Ⓒ $4 \times (45 + 60)$

  Ⓓ $6 + (45 + 60)$

Think It Through

For **example 5**, use the information given in the sign to interpret the expression.

Read the expression. *Multiply 6 times 42, then add 30.* You know that $42 is the cost to rent the chipper for an hour. Multiplying 6 times $42 gives the cost to rent the chipper for 6 hours. Adding $30 includes the delivery fee.

For **example 6**, you do not need to make any calculations to show 4 times the perimeter.

The expression $2 \times (45 + 60)$ gives the perimeter. Multiply this expression by 4 to find 4 times the perimeter. Use brackets to show that the entire expression is multiplied by 4.

$$\boxed{} \times [2 \times (45 + 60)]$$

GO ON →

1 A number y is 3 times greater than a number x. Which equation shows this relationship?

Ⓐ $y = 3 + x$

Ⓑ $y = 3x$

Ⓒ $3y = x$

Ⓓ $y + 3 = x$

2 What is the value of $20 - 5d$ when $d = 3$?

Answer: _____

3 Basheera is 4 years older than Dakota. The variable b stands for Basheera's age. Which expression stands for Dakota's age?

Ⓐ $4b$ Ⓒ $b + 4$

Ⓑ $4 - b$ Ⓓ $b - 4$

4 Write an expression for this phrase. Use n for the unknown number.

a number decreased by 5

Answer: _____

5 Choose the expression that represents this phrase:

a number increased by 4

Ⓐ $x + 4$ Ⓒ $x - 4$

Ⓑ $\frac{4}{x}$ Ⓓ $4x$

6 What is the value of $w - 6$ when $w = 10$?

Ⓐ 16

Ⓑ 4

Ⓒ 14

Ⓓ 2

7 Pamela is planning a quilt. She decides to double the width, w. Write an expression to show the new width.

Answer: _____

8 Choose the equation that represents this sentence:

6 less than 2 times a number equals 4.

Ⓐ $6 - 2n = 4$

Ⓑ $6 = 2n + 4$

Ⓒ $2n - 6 = 4$

Ⓓ $n - 6 = 2 \times 4$

9 Lupe's dog is 10 inches taller than Sarah's dog. The variable s stands for the height of Sarah's dog. Which expression stands for the height of Lupe's dog?

Ⓐ $10s$

Ⓑ $10 - s$

Ⓒ $s + 10$

Ⓓ $s - 10$

Analyzing Patterns and Relationships

Use these sequences for **examples 7** and **8**.

Pattern: Start at 0 and add 5:
0, 5, 10, 15, 20, 25, . . .

Pattern: Start at 0 and add 10:
0, 10, 20, 30, 40, 50, . . .

7 Which statement compares the corresponding terms of the two patterns?

Ⓐ Each *Add 10* term is twice the corresponding *Add 5* term.

Ⓑ Each *Add 5* term is twice the corresponding *Add 10* term.

Ⓒ Each *Add 10* term is 5 times the corresponding *Add 5* term.

Ⓓ Each *Add 5* term is 5 times the corresponding *Add 10* term.

Step-By-Step

For **example 7**, compare each pair of corresponding terms.

Add 5:   0, 5, 10, 15, 20, 25, . . .
          →   →   →   →   →   →
Add 10: 0, 10, 20, 30, 40, 50, . . .

1 Look for ways to describe the relationship between pairs of terms. Start with 5 and 10.

Adding 5 to the first term gives the second term: $5 + 5 = 10$.

Multiplying the first term times 2 gives the second term: $2 \times 5 = 10$.

2 Look for ways to describe the relationship between 10 and 20.

Adding 10 to the first term gives the second term: $10 + 10 = 20$.

Multiplying the first term times 2 gives the second term: $2 \times 10 = 20$.

3 Which relationship is true for both pairs of numbers?

Multiplying the *Add* ▢ term times 2 gives the *Add* ▢ term.

4 Check other pairs of corresponding terms to see if the *Add 10* term is always twice the *Add 5* term then select the correct answer.

Think It Through

For **example 8**, think about the relationship between the rules. Adding 10 is adding 2 times 5.

8 Why is each *Add 10* term 2 times the corresponding *Add 5* term?

Answer: _____

_____

_____

GO ON

10 What is the next number in this pattern?

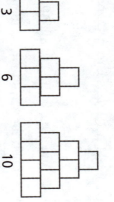

1   3   6   10

Answer: _____

11 Which sequence can be created using the rule *Divide by 2*?

Ⓐ 10, 20, 40, 80, . . .

Ⓑ 90, 80, 70, 60, . . .

Ⓒ 80, 40, 20, 10, . . .

Ⓓ 2, 12, 22, 32, . . .

12 Which is the rule for this sequence?

80, 75, 77, 72, 74, 69, 71, . . .

Ⓐ *Subtract 5*

Ⓑ *Subtract 5, Add 2*

Ⓒ *Add 2*

Ⓓ *Subtract 2, Add 5*

13 Start at 0 and create a pattern using the rule *Add 7*.

Answer: _____

Unit 1 Application

9 **Part A:** Write a numerical expression for: *five times the difference between 10 and 7.*

Step 1

I realize that I must subtract before I can multiply because I have been asked to find "five times the difference."

So, I need to use parentheses to show that subtraction will come before the multiplication.

The full expression is _____.

Step 2

Part B: Evaluate the expression. Show your work.

Answer: _____

Part C: Cearra solved her expression by multiplying 5 by 7, then subtracting 10. Explain her error.

Explanation: _____
_____

Step-By-Step

Plan how you will solve each step of the problem.

My Plan: I will read the question carefully and put it in my own words in order to fully understand what is being asked.

Part A

1 I need to think about the order of operations and determine which operation, subtraction or multiplication, needs to come first. I remember that I might need to use parentheses.

Part B

2 I know that *evaluate* is a math word that means "solve." I need to solve the expression I wrote. I will need to follow the order of operations to make sure I get the correct answer.

Part C

3 I must think about incorrect ways of doing this problem to try to figure out what Cearra does not understand. To do this, I could think about how I correctly completed the problem and what procedures I used. Then, I might think about ways in which someone would do those steps differently.

14 Part A: Evaluate this expression.

$$(19 + 1) \div 4$$

Answer: _____

Part B: Write the following as a numerical expression and evaluate: *The difference between 19 and 1 divided by 4.*

Answer: _____

Explanation: _____

Part C: Explain why Part A has a different answer than Part B.

Answer: _____

15 Part A: Elisa bought a sweater and a matching scarf for her mom, her sister, and her friend. The sweaters cost $40 each and scarves cost $10 each. Write an algebraic expression that represents the total cost.

Answer: _____

Part B: Evaluate the expression.

Answer: _____

16 Part A: Create a pattern by starting at the number 0 and using the rule *Add 4*. Write the numbers in this sequence up to the number 40.

Answer: _____

Part B: Create a pattern by starting at the number 0 and using the rule *Add 8*. Write the numbers in this sequence up to the number 40.

Answer: _____

Part C: Explain why the sequence in Part A contains more numbers than the sequence in Part B.

Explanation: _____

Go for it!

Test Practice 1: Algebraic Thinking

Estimated time: 25 minutes

Directions: Answer each question.

1 Which expression can Jake evaluate to find the cost of 3 pairs of socks that cost $8 each and 2 shirts that cost $18 each?

Ⓐ $(3 + 2) \times (8 + 18)$

Ⓑ $(3 \times 2) + (8 \times 18)$

Ⓒ $(3 \times 8) \times (2 \times 18)$

Ⓓ $(3 \times 8) + (2 \times 18)$

2 Jake's grandfather is 4 times Jake's current age. If the variable a stands for Jake's current age, what expression stands for his grandfather's age?

Ⓐ $a + 4$ Ⓒ $a - 4$

Ⓑ $4 - a$ Ⓓ $4a$

3 Evaluate this expression.

$$9 + [6 \times (18 - 15)] \div 2$$

Answer: _____

4 The area of a triangle can be calculated using the expression $(52 \times 31) \div 2$. Write an expression that can be used to find 3 times the area of the triangle?

Answer: _____

5 Which question can be answered by evaluating the expression below?

$$(14 \times 8) - 30$$

Ⓐ How much profit did Amy earn if she sold 14 bracelets for $8 each and materials cost $30?

Ⓑ What is the total price for 14 bracelets at $8 each plus a necklace for $30?

Ⓒ What is the total cost of 14 bracelets and necklaces if each necklace costs $30 and each bracelet costs $8?

Ⓓ How much change will Amy get from $30 if she buys a necklace for $14 and a bracelet for $8?

6 What is the value of this expression?

$$16 - \{4 + [15 \div (2 + 3)] \times 2\}$$

Answer: _____

7 John bought 5 people each a scarf for $16 and a pair of gloves for $24. Which expression did he use to find the total cost?

Ⓐ $5 \times (16 \times 24)$

Ⓑ $5 \times (16 + 24)$

Ⓒ $5 + (16 \times 24)$

Ⓓ $5 + (16 + 24)$

GO ON

8 Olivia started at 10 and wrote a sequence using the rule *Add 12*. Which sequence did she write?

  Ⓐ 12, 22, 32, 42, 52,...
  Ⓑ 12, 24, 36, 48, 60,...
  Ⓒ 10, 20, 30, 40, 50,...
  Ⓓ 10, 22, 34, 46, 58,...

9 Which expression shows a number 7 times greater than 362 + 45?

  Ⓐ 7 × (362 + 45)
  Ⓑ (362 × 45) + 7
  Ⓒ (362 × 7) + (45 + 7)
  Ⓓ 7 + (362 + 45)

10 Shannon subtracted 18 from 90 and then divided by the sum of 4 and 5. Write the expression she used.

Answer: _____

11 Brayton bicycled 4 times as far as Bob bicycled. Bob bicycled *m* miles. Which expression shows how far Brayton bicycled?

  Ⓐ *m* + 4
  Ⓑ *m* − 4
  Ⓒ *m* ÷ 4
  Ⓓ *m* × 4

12 What is the value of the expression (45 ÷ 9) × 3 − 2 × 6?

Answer: _____

13 Which expression can be used to find the value of *n* nickels and *d* dimes?

  Ⓐ (5 × *n*) + (10 × *d*)
  Ⓑ (5 + 10) × (*n* + *d*)
  Ⓒ (5 + 10) × (*n* × *d*)
  Ⓓ (5 × *d*) + (10 × *n*)

14 Start at 0 and write a sequence for each of these rules:

          Add 3   *Add 9*

Add 3 _____

Add 9 _____

Describe the relationship between the corresponding terms in the two sequences.

Answer: _____

Number Sense

1 Multiplying and Dividing by Powers of Ten **[5.NBT.2]**
2 Exponents and Powers of Ten **[5.NBT.2]**
3 Reading and Writing Decimals **[5.NBT.3.a]**
4 Expanded Form **[5.NBT.1, 5.NBT.3.a]**
5 Comparing Decimals **[5.NBT.3.b]**
6 Rounding Decimals **[5.NBT.4]**

Unit 2 Application **[5.NBT.1 5.NBT.3.a, 5.NBT.3.b]**

Directions: Answer each question.

Multiplying and Dividing by Powers of Ten

1 There are 1,000 milliliters in a liter. How many milliliters are there in 5.775 liters?

Answer: _____ milliliters

Step-By-Step

To change liters to milliliters in **example 1**, you multiply the 5.775 liters by 1,000.

1 Count the number of zeros in 1,000.

There are ☐ zeros.

2 Move the decimal point three places to the right to multiply by 1,000.

5.775↷

$5.775 \times 1000 = $ ☐

Multiplying by Powers of Ten

Count the number of zeros. Move the decimal point **right** that number of places.

$$\$5.00 \times 100 = \$500$$

Dividing by Powers of Ten

Count the number of zeros. Move the decimal point **left** that number of places.

$$\$5.00 \div 100 = \$0.05$$

Multiplying and Dividing by Powers of Ten

2 A meter is 100 centimeters. How many meters are equal to 712 centimeters?

Answer: _____ meters

Think It Through

To change centimeters to meters in **example 2**, divide 712 by 100. There are 2 zeros in 100. To divide 712 by 100, move the decimal point two places to the left.

Exponents and Powers of Ten

3 Write 100,000 in exponential form.

Answer: _____

Powers of Ten

Exponential Form	Standard Form
10^4	10,000
10^3	1,000
10^2	100
10^1	10
10^0	1

Think It Through

Powers of ten such as 100,000 in **example 3** can be written with 10 as repeated factors.

$$100,000 = 10 \times 10 \times 10 \times 10 \times 10$$

The number of times ten is used as a factor is the power of 10. It is the same as the number of zeros in the number.

To write 100,000 in exponential form, count the number of zeros. Then write 10 as the base and 5 as the exponent.

$$100,000 = 10^{\boxed{}}$$

---

4 Write 10^6 in standard form.

Answer: _____

Think It Through

For **example 4**, the number of zeros in the standard form number is given by the exponent.

To write 10^6 in standard form, write a 1 followed by 6 zeros.

Another Way

To write 10^6 in standard form, you can multiply six 10s:

$$10 \times 10 \times 10 \times 10 \times 10 \times 10 = 1,000,000$$

Try It

1 What is the value of 10^6?

Answer: _____

2 Which expression equals 100?

  Ⓐ $10 + 10$

  Ⓑ 10^4

  Ⓒ 10^3

  Ⓓ 10^2

3 The area of a square equals the square of the length of one side. How many square feet are there in the area of a square with a side of 10 feet?

  Ⓐ 2×10

  Ⓑ $10 \times 10 \times 10$

  Ⓒ 10^2

  Ⓓ 2^{10}

4 Write 10^6 as repeated factors.

Answer: _____

5 What is 10^3?

  Ⓐ 100   Ⓒ 500

  Ⓑ 300   Ⓓ 1,000

6 A liter is the same as 1,000 milliliters. How many milliliters are there in 5.6 liters?

Answer: _____ milliliters

7 3,750 milliliters is equal to

  Ⓐ 3.75 liters.

  Ⓑ 37.5 liters.

  Ⓒ 375 liters.

  Ⓓ 3,750 liters.

GO ON

5 Which number is *four million, three hundred six, and twenty-one thousandths?*

   Ⓐ 4,306,020.001

   Ⓑ 4,300,621

   Ⓒ 4,000,306.021

   Ⓓ 4,000,300.621

Step-By-Step

Example 5 gives the number in word form. You need to decide which answer is the **standard form** of the number. A place-value chart can help you by showing you the value of each digit.

1 Read the number and write each digit in its place. Write 4 in the millions place, 3 in the hundreds place, and 6 in the ones place. For 21 thousandths, write 2 in the hundredths place, and 1 in the thousandths place.

2 Fill in the blank spaces with zeros to complete the number.

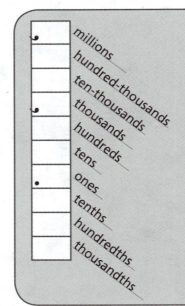

millions	,	hundred-thousands	ten-thousands	thousands	,	hundreds	tens	ones	.	tenths	hundredths	thousandths

Remember . . .

Numbers are arranged in groups of three places, or **periods**. A comma separates each period, and that comma tells you when to say the period name.

8,072,015

eight million, seventy-two thousand, fifteen

We use a decimal point to separate the part of a number that is less than one. A decimal point is read as *and*.

2.009

two and nine thousandths

Reading and Writing Decimals

6 What is the word form for 3.052?

Answer: _____

Step-By-Step

1 Write the number to the left of the decimal point, or 3, in words.

_____

2 Write *and* for the decimal point.

_____

3 Find the place value of the digit farthest to the right. For 3.052, the 2 is in thousandths place. Write 52 in words and then write *thousandths.*

Three and fifty-two
thousandths

Try It

8 What is the place value of 8 in the number 2,364.0087?

Ⓐ thousands
Ⓑ hundreds
Ⓒ hundredths
Ⓓ thousandths

9 What digit is in the ten-thousands place in the number 2,568,902.14?

Ⓐ 5
Ⓑ 6
Ⓒ 9
Ⓓ 4

10 Write the word form for 5.362.

Answer: _____

11 Which number is *twenty-seven million, five hundred thousand, twenty-six, and four thousandths?*

Ⓐ 27,526.4
Ⓑ 27,005,026.4000
Ⓒ 25,500,026.400
Ⓓ 27,500,026.004

7 What is the standard form for 200,000 + 50,000 + 100 + 90 + 2 + 0.6 + 0.08?

Ⓐ 251,926.08

Ⓑ 250,192.68

Ⓒ 205,192.68

Ⓓ 200,519,268

Step-By-Step

In **example 7**, the number is expressed in **expanded form**. To write the number, find the sum.

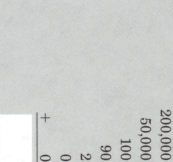

```
  200,000
   50,000
      100
       90
        2
      0.6
+    0.08
_____
```

8 What is 62.507 in expanded form?

Ⓐ 60 + 2 + 0.5 + 0.07

Ⓑ 60 + 2 + 0.05 + 0.007

Ⓒ 60 + 2 + 0.5 + 0.007

Ⓓ 60,000 + 2,000 + 500 + 7

Step-By-Step

For **example 8**, each place in the number has a value. To find it, mentally multiply the digit times the place value. If a place has zero in it, its value is zero and is not shown in the expanded form.

1 6 is in tens place; 6 × 10 = ☐

2 2 is in ones place; 2 × 1 = ☐

3 5 is in _____ place; 5 × 0.1 = 0.5

4 7 is in _____ 0.007

5 7 is in _____ place; 7 × 0.001 = ☐

5 Write the numbers as a sum.

60 + 2 + ☐ + ☐

Forms of Numbers

Standard form: 940,602.38

Word form: *Nine hundred forty thousand, six hundred two and thirty-eight hundredths*

Expanded form: 900,000 + 40,000 + 600 + 2 + 0.3 + 0.08

Place Value

Each place value is 10 times more than the place to its right and 10 times less than the place to its left.

Ten-thousands	Thousands	Hundreds	Tens	Ones	Tenths	Hundredths	Thousandths
10,000	1,000	100	10	1	0.1	0.01	0.001

Try It

12 Which is the number for *two hundred five and six hundredths?*

Ⓐ 2,056   © 205.06

Ⓑ 205.6   Ⓓ 205.006

13 Which shows 72.05 in expanded notation?

Ⓐ 70 + 2 + 0.05
Ⓑ 70 + 2 + 0.5
© 70 + 20 + 5
Ⓓ 70 + 0.2 + 0.5

14 What is the expanded form for 520.043?

Ⓐ 500 + 2 + 0.4 + 0.003
Ⓑ 500 + 20 + 0.04 + 0.003
© 500 + 20 + 4 + 3
Ⓓ 5 + 20 + 4 + 3

15 What is the standard form for 2,000 + 500 + 30 + 2 + 0.5 + 0.01?

Answer: _____

Comparing Decimals

9 One ground squirrel weighed 0.492 kilograms. Another weighed 0.485 kilograms. Which answer correctly compares the two decimals?

Ⓐ 0.485 = 0.492
Ⓑ 0.492 > 0.485
© 0.492 < 0.485
Ⓓ 0.485 > 0.492

Step-By-Step

For **example 9**, compare the digits from left to right.

1 Compare each place until you find digits that are different.

0.4<u>9</u>2

0.4<u>8</u>5

Use those digits to decide which number is greater.

9 > 8, so 0.492 ▢ 0.482

2 Choose the answer that correctly compares the decimals.

10 Alvin swam a lap in 13.07 seconds. What was his time to the nearest tenth of a second?

Ⓐ 13

Ⓑ 13.1

Ⓒ 13.7

Ⓓ 14

Remember . . .

When you **round up,** → add 1 to the digit.

When you **round down,** ↓ the digit stays the same.

Step-By-Step

For **example 10,** you will need to round the decimal 13.07 to the nearest tenth.

1 Look at the number. What number is in the tenths place? Zero. So you know that when you round the number, the number in the tenths place will be either 0 or 1.

2 To round, look at the number to the right in the hundredths place. What is that number?

3 When the number in this place is 5 through 9, you increase the number in the place you are rounding to by 1. What number will you write in the tenths place?

4 What is 13.07 rounded to the nearest tenth?

Try It

16 What is 12.2536 rounded to the nearest tenth?

Ⓐ 12.0   Ⓒ 12.3

Ⓑ 12.2   Ⓓ 13.0

17 Round 12.06 to the nearest . . .

whole number: _____

ten: _____

18 Which number can go in the blank so the numbers are ordered from least to greatest?

419.15, _____, 420.202

Ⓐ 418.265

Ⓑ 419.05

Ⓒ 419.4

Ⓓ 420.255

Try It continued

19 The table shows the weights of four dogs.

Dog	Weight (in kilograms)
Snowy	8.32
Bing	7.95
Pal	8.4
Shadow	8.38

Order the dogs from heaviest to lightest. Write the weights below.

Answer: _____

20 Round 12.46 seconds to the nearest tenth of a second.

Answer: _____

11 **Part A:** Explain how to write a number in expanded form.

Step 1

Explanation: _____

_____

Part B: Write the numbers 34.974 and 34.874 in expanded form.

Step 2

34.974 = ____ + ____ + ____ + ____

+ ____ .

34.874 = ____ + ____ + ____ + ____

+ ____ .

Part C: Write an inequality using < or > to compare the two numbers you wrote in expanded form.

Step 3

Answer: _____

Part D: What is the numerical difference between 34.974 and 34.874? Using your knowledge of place value, explain your answer.

Step 4

```
  34.974
- 34.874
_____
```

Explanation: _____

_____

Step-By-Step

Plan how you will solve each step of the problem.

Part A

1 I know that every digit in a number has a value according to its place in the number. I will explain how to use this information to write any number in expanded form.

Part B

2 I can use the explanation I wrote for Part A to complete this task.

I know, for example, that the 3 in the number 34.974 is in the tens place. This means its value is actually 3×10 or 30. I will use this idea to finish Part B for both numbers.

Part C

3 I remember that < means "less than" and > means "greater than."

For this part, I can use either symbol to show a relationship between the two numbers depending upon which number I write first. So, I know there is more than one correct answer for this question.

Part D

4 As shown, I can subtract the two numbers to find their numerical difference.

I could also compare the expanded form of the numbers from Part B to find the difference.

I need to explain how I know my answer is correct using what I know about place value.

21 **Part A:** A piano costs $2,387.99. The storeowner wants to mark down the current price by $100. Which digit in the price should she change?

Answer: _____

Part B: What is the new price of the piano?

Answer: _____

Part C: Round your answer from Part B to the nearest thousand.

Answer: _____

22 **Part A:** If you round the number 4.251 to the nearest hundredth, it becomes 4.25. Write three other numbers that also round to 4.25 when you round them to the nearest hundredth.

Answer: _____

Part B: Explain why the numbers you chose for Part A will round to 4.25.

Explanation: _____

Part C: What is difference between the numbers 4.251 and 4.253? Explain your answer in terms of place value. Relate these two numbers using either < or >.

Answer: _____

23 **Part A:** Alice, Emily, and Rose ran a 100-meter race. Emily finished first, Rose was second, and Alice was third. Match the girls' names to their race times as shown in the chart below:

Name	Time
	20.09 seconds
	20.43 seconds
	19.99 seconds

Part B: Round each finishing time to the nearest tenth of a second and write it above.

Part C: Write a single inequality that relates all three numbers.

Answer: _____

Test Practice 2: Number Sense

Directions: Answer each question.

1 Which choice shows the written form of 16.492?

Ⓐ *sixteen thousand, four hundred ninety-two*

Ⓑ *sixteen and four hundred ninety-two hundredths*

Ⓒ *sixteen and four hundred ninety-two thousandths*

Ⓓ *sixteen, four hundred ninety-two*

2 Which symbol makes this number sentence true?

$$0.03 \,\square\, 0.030$$

Ⓐ =

Ⓑ <

Ⓒ >

Ⓓ ×

3 Rachel bought 4.016 kilograms of cheese. To the nearest hundredth of a kilogram, how much cheese did she buy?

Ⓐ 4.1 kg   Ⓒ 4.02 kg

Ⓑ 4.01 kg   Ⓓ 4.2 kg

4 To find the number of liters in 4,126 milliliters, divide by 1,000. How many liters are there in 4,126 milliliters?

Answer: _____

5 What is the standard form of the number $10 + 6 + 0.4 + 0.007$?

Answer: _____

6 A restaurant earns $10,000 each week. If it continues to earn the same amount of money each week, how much will it earn in 24 weeks?

Ⓐ $24,000

Ⓑ $240,000

Ⓒ $2,400,000

Ⓓ $24,000,000

7 Which statement is true?

Ⓐ 51.605 = 51.65

Ⓑ 51.605 > 51.65

Ⓒ 51.605 < 51.65

Ⓓ 51.650 > 51.65

8 Lateesha hiked the trail of a wilderness area. According to the map, the trail is 3.45 miles long. How far did she hike rounded to the nearest tenth?

Ⓐ 0.3 mi   Ⓒ 0.5 mi

Ⓑ 0.4 mi   Ⓓ 3.5 mi

9 What is the value of the digit 7 in the decimal 60.758?

Ⓐ 7 tenths

Ⓑ 70

Ⓒ 7 hundredths

Ⓓ 700

10 Which is the number for *two hundred five and six hundredths?*

Ⓐ 2,056
Ⓑ 205.6
Ⓒ 205.06
Ⓓ 205.006

11 What is the place value of 8 in the number 2,364.087?

Ⓐ thousands
Ⓑ hundreds
Ⓒ hundredths
Ⓓ thousandths

12 Which answer shows the exponential notation for 10,000?

Ⓐ 10^4
Ⓑ 10^5
Ⓒ 10^6
Ⓓ 10^7

13 Which shows 72.05 in expanded notation?

Ⓐ 70 + 2 + 0.05
Ⓑ 70 + 2 + 0.5
Ⓒ 70 + 20 + 5
Ⓓ 70 + 0.2 + 0.5

14 Which number is less than 0.07?

Ⓐ 0.065
Ⓑ 0.075
Ⓒ 0.705
Ⓓ 0.65

15 Write 1,000 in exponential notation.

Answer: _____

16 What is the word form of the number 5.602?

Ⓐ *five and six hundred two thousandths*
Ⓑ *five and sixty-two thousandths*
Ⓒ *fifty-six and two hundredths*
Ⓓ *fifty-six and two thousandths*

17 0.56 × 1,000 =

Ⓐ 5.6
Ⓑ 5.06
Ⓒ 560
Ⓓ 56,000

18 Choose the standard form of the decimal *forty-six thousandths.*

Ⓐ 0.46
Ⓑ 0.406
Ⓒ 0.046
Ⓓ 4.006

19 Write the standard form number for 10^5.

Answer: _____

20 Explain how to move the decimal point to divide 324.567 by 100.

Answer: _____

STOP

Points Earned/Total = _____/20

MATH Unit 3

Operations with Whole Numbers and Decimals

1 Multiplying Whole Numbers [5.NBT.5]
2 Relating Multiplication and Division [5.NBT.6]
3 Dividing Whole Numbers [5.NBT.6]
4 Adding and Subtracting Decimals [5.NBT.7]
5 Multiplying and Dividing Decimals [5.NBT.7]
6 Multi-Step Problems [5.NBT.7]

Unit 3 Application [5.NBT.5, 5.NBT.7]

Multiplying Whole Numbers

Step-By-Step

To find the total number of pens for **example 1**, you need to multiply.

1 Set up the problem by writing one number below the other and lining up the digits.

2 Multiply 258 by the value of the digit in the ones place (4). Then multiply 258 by the value of the digit in the tens place (40) and by the value of the digit in the hundreds place (100). Add to find the answer.

$$\begin{array}{r} 258 \\ \times\ 144 \end{array}$$

$$\begin{array}{r} 258 \\ \times\ 144 \\ \hline 1032 \\ 10320 \\ +\ 25800 \\ \hline \end{array}$$
multiply by ones place
multiply by tens place
multiply by hundreds place
add

Directions: Answer each question.

1 A factory shipped 258 cartons of pens. There are 144 pens in each carton. How many pens did the factory ship?

Ⓐ 2,322
Ⓑ 4,644
Ⓒ 36,152
Ⓓ 37,152

Properties of Operations

Use these **properties of operations** to help you perform computations more effectively.

Commutative Property	**Associative Property**	**Distributive Property**
You can add or multiply numbers in any order.	You can group addends or factors in different ways.	The product of a sum or difference equals the sum or difference of two products.
$24 + 45 = 45 + 24$	$6 + (4 + 8) = (6 + 4) + 8$	$3 \times (4 + 6) = 3 \times 4 + 3 \times 6$
$32 \times 15 = 15 \times 32$	$(9 \times 2) \times 5 = 9 \times (2 \times 5)$	$5 \times (8 - 2) = 5 \times 8 - 5 \times 2$

Relating Multiplication and Division

2 Which belongs to the same fact family as

$$84 \div 7 = 12?$$

- (A) $6 \times 14 = 84$
- (B) $12 - 7 = 5$
- (C) $84 + 12 = 96$
- (D) $12 \times 7 = 84$

Think It Through

For **example 2**, you can use a **fact family** to find a related fact. Multiplication and division are inverse operations. They "undo" each other.

In this diagram, there are 12 dots in 7 rows for a total of 84 dots.

This **fact family** is represented by the diagram.

$7 \times 12 = 84 \qquad 84 \div 12 = 7$

$12 \times 7 = 84 \qquad 84 \div 7 = 12$

---

3 Find the value of p in the equation below.

$$p \times 6 = 96$$

   Ⓐ 576   Ⓒ 36

   Ⓑ 90   Ⓓ 16

Opposite Operations

Use **opposite operations** to get a variable alone on one side of an equation. You must perform the same operation on both sides of the equation.

To undo addition, *subtract*.

To undo subtraction, *add*.

To undo multiplication, *divide*.

To undo division, *multiply*.

Try It

1 A mason is building a wall 22 bricks tall. He needs 128 bricks for each row. How many bricks does he need in all? Show your work.

Answer: _____

2 For Arbor Day, 45 different ecology clubs raised $250 each to pay for new tree plantings. How much money did they raise in all?

Answer: _____

Step-By-Step

In **example 3**, you are to find the value of the **variable** p.

1 The operation used in this equation is multiplication. Use the opposite operation to get the variable alone on the left side of the equation.

$$p \times 6 = 96$$
$$p \times (6 \div 6) = 96 \div 6$$
$$p \times (1) = 96 \div 6$$
$$p = \boxed{}$$

2 To check, substitute your answer for p in the original equation.

$$p \times 6 = 96$$
$$\boxed{} \times 6 = 96$$

Does your answer check out?

3 Which belongs to the same fact family as $6 \times 14 = 84$?

   Ⓐ $14 - 6 = 8$

   Ⓑ $84 \div 14 = 6$

   Ⓒ $84 - 14 = 70$

   Ⓓ $14 + 6 = 20$

4 Write three number sentences that belong to the same fact family as $80 \div 5 = 16$.

Answer: _____

5 Find the value of n in the equation below.

$$n \times 15 = 90$$

Answer: _____

Dividing Whole Numbers

4 There are 32 apricots in a box. Mr. Vance boxed 1,472 apricots. How many boxes did he fill?

Answer: _____

Remainders

Sometimes, there will be a number left over when you divide. It is called a **remainder**.

Remainders can be represented using the letter R, or they can be expressed as a fraction.

$$2 \text{ R } 33 \qquad 2\frac{33}{46}$$
$$46\overline{)125} \qquad 46\overline{)125}$$

Checking Division by Multiplying

Check division by multiplying the quotient times the divisor and then adding the remainder.

$$\begin{array}{r} 15 \text{ R } 3 \\ 8\overline{)123} \end{array} \qquad \begin{array}{r} 15 \\ \times\ 8 \\ \hline 120 \\ +\ 3 \\ \hline 123 \end{array}$$

Step-By-Step

For **example 4**, let b be the number of boxes. Solve the equation $b = 1472 \div 32$.

1 Write the division problem and use compatible numbers to estimate.

$$32\overline{)1472} \text{ is about } 30\overline{)1500}^{\,50}$$

2 Use 5 as the first digit in the quotient. Multiply 5×32.

$$\begin{array}{r} 5 \\ 32\overline{)1472} \\ 160 \end{array} \qquad \begin{array}{l} 160 \text{ is greater than 147,} \\ \text{so 5 is too big.} \end{array}$$

3 Try 4.

$$\begin{array}{r} 4 \\ 32\overline{)1472} \\ -\ 128 \\ \hline 192 \end{array} \qquad \begin{array}{l} \text{Multiply } 4 \times 32. \\ \text{Subtract and bring down the 2.} \end{array}$$

4 Use compatible numbers to estimate $192 \div 32$.

$$180 \div 30 = \boxed{}$$

5 Try 6 as the second digit in the quotient.

$$\begin{array}{r} 46 \\ 32\overline{)1472} \\ -\ 128 \\ \hline 192 \\ -\ \boxed{} \\ \hline \end{array} \qquad \text{Multiply } 6 \times 32.$$

6 $b = $ _____

GO ON

6 Estimate the first digit of the quotient in the problem 6,427 ÷ 81.

Answer: _____

7 How long does a 676-mile trip take at an average speed of 52 miles per hour?

Ⓐ 13 hr   Ⓒ 14 hr

Ⓑ 13.5 hr   Ⓓ 624 hr

8 3,577 ÷ 42 =

Ⓐ 84 R 49   Ⓒ 85 R 17

Ⓑ 85 R 7   Ⓓ 87 R 23

9 Peter chooses a 560-page book for his book report. He plans to read 35 pages per day. How long will it take him to read the book?

Answer: _____

Adding and Subtracting Decimals

5 Find the sum.

0.4 + 0.35

Ⓐ 0.39
Ⓑ 0.75
Ⓒ 39
Ⓓ 75

Modeling Addition on a Hundreds Chart

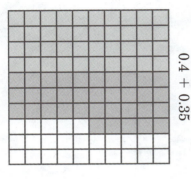

0.4 + 0.35

Step-By-Step

You can add the decimals in **example 5** just like you add whole numbers.

1 Line up the decimal points to write the addition problem vertically. Add a 0 to 4 tenths to help you line up the decimals.

```
  0.40
+ 0.35
```

2 Then add. Remember to write a 0 in the ones place followed by a decimal point.

```
  0.40
+ 0.35
```

Step-By-Step

Subtract the decimals in **example 6** just like you subtract whole numbers.

1 Line up the decimal points to write the subtraction vertically. Write 8 tenths as 80 hundredths to make it easier to line up the decimals.

$$\begin{array}{r} 0.80 \\ -\ 0.33 \\ \hline \end{array}$$

2 Then subtract. Remember to write a 0 in the ones place followed by a decimal point.

$$\begin{array}{r} 0.80 \\ -\ 0.33 \\ \hline \end{array}$$

Step-By-Step

In **example 7**, the factors have a total of 2 decimal places. There will be 2 decimal places in the product.

1 Multiply as if the numbers were both whole numbers.

$$\begin{array}{r} 407 \\ \times\ 23 \\ \hline 1221 \\ +\ 8140 \\ \hline \end{array}$$

2 Place the decimal point in the product.

9 3 6 1

Adding and Subtracting Decimals

6 Subtract.

0.8 − 0.33

Ⓐ 0.25   © 0.47

Ⓑ 0.35   Ⓓ 0.53

Modeling Subtraction on a Hundreds Chart

0.8 − 0.33

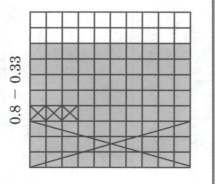

Multiplying and Dividing Decimals

7 23 × 4.07 =

Ⓐ 9.361   © 9.361

Ⓑ 93.61   Ⓓ 9,361

Remember . . .

When you multiply decimals, the number of decimal places in the product is the sum of the number of decimal places in the factors.

1.003 ⟶ 3 decimal places

30.06 ⟶ + 2 decimal places

30.15018 ⟶ 5 decimal places

8 A flower bed with a width of 1.2 meters has an area of 4.08 square meters. What is the length of the flower bed?

- Ⓐ 34 m
- Ⓒ 3.4 m
- Ⓑ 3.04 m
- Ⓓ 0.34 m

Remember . . .

When dividing by a decimal, first convert the divisor to a whole number by moving the decimal point. You must move the decimal point in the dividend the same number of places.

$$0.8\overline{)2.88} \qquad 8\overline{)28.8}$$

Step-By-Step

In **example 8**, you are dividing by a decimal.

1 Change the divisor to a whole number. Move the decimal point one place to the right in both the divisor and the dividend.

2 Divide as normal. Be sure to put the decimal point in the proper place in the quotient.

$$
\begin{array}{r}
3. \\
12\overline{)40.8} \\
-36 \\
\end{array}
$$

Try It

10 4.2 × 0.06 =

Answer: _____

11 George sold his comic book collection. He packed the books in three boxes that weighed 0.7 lb, 2.3 lb, and 5.25 lb. What was the total weight of the boxes?

- Ⓐ 5.55 lb
- Ⓒ 8.25 lb
- Ⓑ 7.25 lb
- Ⓓ 9.25 lb

12 0.587 − 0.03 =

Answer: _____

13 Flora is mailing 400 pairs of plastic sunglasses that each weigh 0.08 kg. How much will the entire shipment of sunglasses weigh?

Answer: _____

14 Jake made 15.2 liters of punch for a family picnic. After the picnic was over, there were 3.75 liters of punch left. How much punch was used at the picnic?

Answer: _____

15 0.8 + 0.04 + 0.2 + 0.06 =

- Ⓐ 0.11
- Ⓒ 0.2
- Ⓑ 1.1
- Ⓓ 2

Answer: _____

16 Lonnie estimates he can bicycle at an average speed of 15 miles per hour. At this rate, how far can he go in 0.7 hours?

17 Alexa wants 20.5 liters of blueberries to make jam. She picked 7.3 liters on Friday and 4.25 liters on Saturday. How many more liters does she need to pick?

- Ⓐ 8.95 L
- Ⓒ 11.05 L
- Ⓑ 9.05 L
- Ⓓ 11.55 L

Open-Ended Practice

Some tests include questions in which you must write an explanation of how you solved a problem. You may also be asked to show your work, draw graphs, or make diagrams. The example below will give you practice answering such questions.

Multi-Step Problems

9 Paula left home with $20. She now has $4.62 because she bought 2 pounds of cashews. How much did she pay for 1 pound of cashews?

Show OR describe each step of your work, even if you did it in your head ("mental math") or used a calculator.

Write an explanation stating the mathematical reason(s) why you chose each of your steps.

Explanation: _____

_____

_____

_____

_____

Think It Through

Review what you know and make a plan to solve **example 9**. Then show your work and explain your thinking. Write clearly and label each step as in the example below.

My plan: *I know Paula had $20 and now has $4.62. I know she bought 2 pounds of cashews. I will find the amount Paula spent for 2 pounds of cashews. Then I will find the price of 1 pound of cashews.*

Step 1: Find the price of 2 pounds of cashews.

$$\begin{array}{r} \$20.00 \\ -\ 4.62 \\ \hline \$15.38 \end{array}$$

Step 2: Find the price of 1 pound of cashews.

$$\begin{array}{r} \$\ 7.69 \\ 2\overline{)\$15.38} \\ -\ 14 \\ \hline 13 \\ -\ 12 \\ \hline 18 \\ -\ 18 \\ \hline 0 \end{array}$$

Explanation: *I first found the price of 2 pounds of cashews by subtracting the amount Paula has left from the $20 she started with. 2 pounds of cashews cost $15.38. I found the price of 1 pound of cashews by dividing $15.38 by 2.*

10 **Part A:** Maria earns $30 per hour at her job. She works 8 hours a day, 5 days a week. How much money does she earn in a week?

Step 1

$$\frac{}{\text{earnings per hour}} \times \frac{}{\text{hours she works per day}} \times \frac{}{\text{days per week}} = \frac{}{\text{earnings per week}}$$

Maria earns _____ per week.

Part B: How many weeks are there in a year? Appropriately round the number of weeks in a year so you can use mental math to estimate Maria's yearly pay. What is Maria's approximate yearly pay?

Step 2

$$50 \times \frac{}{\text{earnings per week}} = \frac{}{}$$

Marie earns about _____ per year.

Part C: Calculate the exact amount of money Maria earns every year.

Step 3

$$\frac{}{\text{number of weeks}} \times \frac{}{\text{earnings per week}} = \frac{}{}$$

Marie earns exactly _____ per year.

Step-By-Step

Plan how you will solve each step of the problem.

Part A

1 I need to figure out how much money Maria earns each week. I know

- how much she earns per hour,
- how many hours per day she works,
- and how many days she goes to work each week.

I multiply to figure out the how much Maria makes each day, and then multiply again to calculate Maria's weekly salary.

Part B

2 I know there are 52 weeks in a year. To make my mental math easier, I can round this number to 50 weeks and multiply it by the amount of money Maria earns each week. This process will estimate her yearly pay.

Part C

3 I remember that using the standard algorithm means to multiply the actual numbers using pencil and paper rather than mental math.

I used an estimate for the number of weeks, so that is the number that will change.

Unit 3 Application continued

Part D: Compare the number you calculated in Part B with the number for Part C. Which is less? Is it reasonable that one number is less than the other? Why or why not?

Step 4

Explanation: _____

_____

_____

_____

_____

Part D

4 I see that the actual number I calculated is more than my estimate. I look back at my rounding and use my mathematical knowledge to determine if that is reasonable and why.

18 Part A: Mark has 3 quarters, 2 nickels, and 5 pennies. How much money does he have altogether?

Answer: _____

Part B: Mark divides his money equally into four shares. How much is in each share? Is there any money left over? If so, how much?

Answer: _____

Part B: Multiply 20 by 2.5 to verify your answer. Show your work.

19 Part A: Laura rides her bike at a rate of 20 miles per hour. How many miles can she ride in $2\frac{1}{2}$ hours? Draw a diagram to illustrate your answer.

Answer: _____

Part C: Write an equation to represent how long it takes Laura to ride her bike 60 miles. Use the variable h to represent the number of hours.

Answer: _____

20 Part A: At the beginning of his day, Fernando had $45.54. He bought three magazines that each had the same price. After buying the magazines, he had $30.57 left. How much did each magazine cost?

Answer: _____

Part B: Explain how you found your answer to Part A.

Explanation: _____

Go for it!

Test Practice 3: Operations with Whole Numbers and Decimals

Directions: Answer each question.

1 Jake made 15.2 liters of punch for a family picnic. After the picnic was over, there were 3.75 liters of punch left. How much punch was used at the picnic?

Ⓐ 6.77 L   Ⓒ 12.55 L

Ⓑ 11.45 L   Ⓓ 18.95 L

2 Carlos bought 86.2 grams of walnuts and 52.89 grams of chopped almonds. How many grams of nuts did he buy altogether?

Ⓐ 615.1 g   Ⓒ 139.09 g

Ⓑ 138.91 g   Ⓓ 139.9 g

3 Alexa needs 20.5 liters of blueberries to make jam. She picked 7.3 liters on Friday and 4.25 liters on Saturday. How many more liters does she need to pick?

Answer: _____

4 Will, Sam, and Cierra earned $78.75 washing cars. If they share the money equally, how much will each person get? Show your work below.

Answer: _____

5 Romeo uses 8 wheels on each of the toy trucks he builds. He has a total of 728 wheels. How many toy trucks can he build?

Ⓐ 920

Ⓑ 91

Ⓒ 89

Ⓓ 9

6 Elsa is printing 350 copies of her book. The book is 128 pages long. How many sheets of paper does she need?

Ⓐ 4,480

Ⓑ 37,800

Ⓒ 43,800

Ⓓ 44,800

7 Flip-flops cost $8.49 a pair. What is the cost of 4 pairs of flip-flops?

Answer: _____

8 $6,399 \div 81 = ?$ Show your work below.

Answer: _____

GO ON

9 Anthony bought a drill for $147.80 and drill bits for $14.88. How much change did he get from $200?

Answer: _____

10 Subtract.

$35.19
− 18.37

Ⓐ $16.18
Ⓑ $16.82
Ⓒ $17.18
Ⓓ $23.22

11 Divide. Show your work.

1.2)24

12 Find the product. Show your work.

4216
× 32

Answer: _____

13 Which number correctly completes this equation?

☐ × 8 = 88

Ⓐ 8
Ⓑ 11
Ⓒ 80
Ⓓ 704

14 Juan worked 35.5 hours last week. He earns $22.80 an hour. How much did he earn last week?

Answer: _____

15 What is the value of n in the equation
$5 \times n = 75$?

Ⓐ 5
Ⓑ 15
Ⓒ 70
Ⓓ 375

16 Tickets to a concert cost $36 each. There are 420 seats in the theater. How much will the theater take in if tickets for all 420 seats are sold? Show your work below.

Answer: _____

17 Peter chooses a 560-page book for his book report. He plans to read 35 pages per day.

Part A: How long will it take him to read the book? Show your work. Explain how you got your answer.

Explanation: _____

_____

Part B: If Peter chooses a book that is 140 pages longer and wants to read it in 14 days, how many pages must he read each day? Show your work. Explain how you got your answer.

Explanation: _____

_____

18 The square represents 1 whole. Record the addition shown by the model. Explain your reasoning.

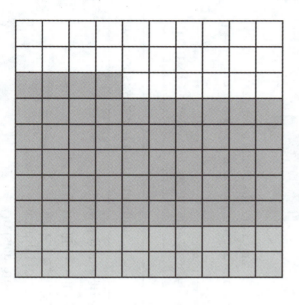

Explanation: _____

_____

STOP

Points Earned/Total = _____/18

Fractions

MATH Unit 4

1 Adding Fractions and Mixed Numbers [5.NF.1, 5.NF.2]
2 Subtracting Fractions and Mixed Numbers [5.NF.1, 5.NF.2]
3 Estimating Sums and Differences [5.NF.2]
4 Division and Fractions [5.NF.3]
5 Multiplying with Fractions and Mixed Numbers [5.NF.4.a, 5.NF.4.b, 5. NF.5.a, 5.NF.F.b, 5.NF.6]
6 Dividing with Fractions [5.NF.7.a, 5.NF.7.b, 5.NF.7.c]
Unit 4 Application [5.NF.1, 5.NF.2]

Directions: Answer each question.

Adding Fractions and Mixed Numbers

1 Julian ate $\frac{3}{8}$ of a pizza for dinner and $\frac{1}{4}$ of the pizza for a snack the next day.

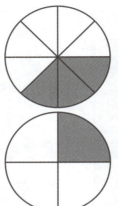

What fraction of the pizza did he eat in all?

Ⓐ $\frac{5}{16}$

Ⓑ $\frac{1}{3}$

Ⓒ $\frac{1}{2}$

Ⓓ $\frac{5}{8}$

Step-By-Step

For **example 1**, add $\frac{3}{8}$ and $\frac{1}{4}$ to find the fraction of the pizza Julian ate.

1 Fractions must have the same denominator before you can add them. Look at the model. You can see that $\frac{1}{4}$ is twice the size of $\frac{1}{8}$. Write an equivalent fraction for $\frac{1}{4}$ that has a denominator of 8.

$$\frac{1}{4} = \frac{1 \times 2}{4 \times 2} = \frac{\boxed{}}{8}$$

2 Let t be the total amount of pizza Julian ate. Write an equation for finding t.

$$t = \frac{3}{8} + \frac{2}{8}$$

3 Add numerators to solve for t.

$$t = \frac{3}{8} + \frac{2}{8} = \frac{3+2}{8} = \frac{\boxed{}}{8}$$

Adding Fractions and Mixed Numbers

2 Hank drew a line that was $4\frac{1}{9}$ inches long. Then he made the line $3\frac{5}{6}$ inches longer. How long was the final line?

Ⓐ $7\frac{6}{15}$ inches

Ⓑ $7\frac{3}{5}$ inches

Ⓒ $7\frac{2}{3}$ inches

Ⓓ $7\frac{17}{18}$ inches

Finding Equivalent Fractions

To find an equivalent fraction, multiply or divide both terms by the same number.

$$\frac{2}{5} \times \frac{4}{4} = \frac{8}{20}$$

Step-By-Step

To answer **example 2**, you need to add $4\frac{1}{9} + 3\frac{5}{6}$. Follow these steps.

1 Since the fraction parts do not have the same denominator, find a common denominator. Write some multiples of both denominators.

9: 9, 18, ____ , ____ , · · ·

6: 6, 12, ____ , ____ , · · ·

2 What is the first multiple that is the same in both lists?

____

3 Rewrite each fraction part as an equivalent fraction with a denominator of 18.

$$\frac{1 \times 2}{9 \times 2} = \frac{2}{18} \qquad \frac{5 \times 3}{6 \times 3} = \frac{15}{18}$$

4 Add the mixed numbers, starting with the fraction parts.

$$\begin{array}{r} 4\frac{2}{18} \\ + 3\frac{15}{18} \\ \hline \end{array}$$

____

Try It

1 $4\frac{3}{10} + 1\frac{3}{10} =$

Ⓐ $4\frac{1}{5}$ Ⓒ $5\frac{3}{5}$

Ⓑ $4\frac{3}{5}$ Ⓓ $6\frac{3}{5}$

2 To make punch for a party, Alice mixed $5\frac{1}{2}$ quarts of lemonade with $2\frac{1}{4}$ quarts of cranberry juice. How much punch did she make?

Answer: _____

GO ON

3 Jermain needs $\frac{9}{10}$ liter of milk. He has $\frac{3}{10}$ liter of milk. What fraction of a liter more does he need?

Answer: _____ liter

Simplifying Fractions

To write a fraction in simplest form, divide the numerator and denominator by their greatest common factor.

$$\frac{16}{20} = \frac{16 \div 4}{20 \div 4} = \frac{4}{5}$$

---

4 Leticia had $1\frac{1}{4}$ yards of ribbon. She used $\frac{3}{4}$ yard for a craft project. How much ribbon does she have left?

- Ⓐ $\frac{3}{4}$ yd
- Ⓑ $\frac{1}{2}$ yd
- Ⓒ $\frac{1}{4}$ yd
- Ⓓ $\frac{1}{8}$ yd

Step-By-Step

For **example 3**, let m be the amount of milk Jermain needs and write a subtraction equation.

1 Write an equation. The amount of milk Jermain needs equals $\frac{9}{10}$ of a liter minus $\frac{3}{10}$ liter.

$$m = \frac{9}{10} - \frac{3}{10}$$

2 Subtract numerators.

$$m = \frac{9}{10} - \frac{3}{10} = \frac{\boxed{}}{10}$$

3 The answer is not in simplest form. Find the greatest common factor of 6 and 10.

Factors of 6: 1, 2, 3, 6

Factors of 10: 1, 2, 5, 10

The greatest common factor is _____

4 Divide the numerator and denominator by the greatest common factor to rewrite the fraction in its simplest form.

$$m = \frac{6}{10} = \frac{6 \div 2}{10 \div 2} = \frac{\boxed{}}{\boxed{}}$$

For **example 4**, you cannot subtract $\frac{3}{4}$ from $\frac{1}{4}$, so you must rewrite $1\frac{1}{4}$ as an improper fraction.

1 Write $1\frac{1}{4}$ as an improper fraction.

$$1\frac{1}{4} = \frac{\boxed{}}{4}$$

2 Subtract.

$$\begin{array}{r} \frac{5}{4} \\ -\frac{3}{4} \\ \hline \boxed{} \end{array}$$

3 Write the answer in simplest form.

$$\frac{2}{4} = \boxed{}$$

Try It

3 A sewing pattern shows that $5\frac{1}{8}$ yards of fabric are needed to make a bathrobe. A matching nightshirt needs only $1\frac{7}{8}$ yards. How much more fabric is needed for the bathrobe than for the nightshirt?

Ⓐ $3\frac{1}{4}$ yd   Ⓒ $4\frac{3}{4}$ yd

Ⓑ $3\frac{3}{8}$ yd   Ⓓ 7 yd

4 $\frac{11}{20} - \frac{3}{20} = ?$

Ⓐ $\frac{2}{5}$ Ⓒ $\frac{3}{10}$

Ⓑ $\frac{13}{20}$ Ⓓ $\frac{4}{5}$

5 $\frac{7}{12} - \frac{3}{16} = ?$

Answer: _____

6 Marcy is practicing for a swimming race. She swam $3\frac{1}{8}$ miles on Friday and $2\frac{1}{2}$ miles on Saturday. How much farther did she swim on Friday?

Answer: _____

7 $8\frac{7}{9} - 4\frac{1}{9} = ?$

Answer: _____

Estimating Sums and Differences

5 Shawna had $4\frac{5}{8}$ yards of fabric. She used $3\frac{1}{8}$ yards for a project. About how much fabric does she have left?

Ⓐ $1\frac{1}{2}$ yards

Ⓑ 2 yards

Ⓒ $2\frac{1}{2}$ yards

Ⓓ 3 yards

Step-By-Step

The word *about* in **example 5** tells you that you do not need an exact answer. You can estimate.

1 Round each amount of fabric to the nearest half yard.

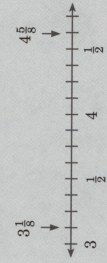

$4\frac{5}{8}$ is about $4\frac{1}{2}$ yards

$3\frac{1}{8}$ is about ☐ yards

2 Subtract the rounded numbers mentally.

$4\frac{1}{2} - 3 = $ ☐

GO ON

6 Eddie added $\frac{1}{3} + \frac{2}{5} = \frac{3}{8}$.

Is his answer reasonable? _____

Another Way to Check

Compare the fractions in the problem to check whether the answer is reasonable.

$$\frac{1}{4} + \frac{3}{5} = \frac{4}{9}$$

The addend $\frac{3}{5}$ is greater than $\frac{1}{2}$. The sum $\frac{4}{9}$ is less than $\frac{1}{2}$. The sum can not be less than an addend, so the answer is not reasonable.

Step-By-Step

For **example 6**, round each fraction to the nearest half to check if the answer is reasonable.

1 Round the fractions.

$\frac{1}{3}$ is about $\frac{1}{2}$

$\frac{2}{5}$ is about ☐

2 Use mental math to add the fractions.

$\frac{1}{2} + \frac{1}{2} = $ ☐

3 Compare the estimate and the answer. Is the answer reasonable?

Division and Fractions

7 Which expression has the same meaning as $\frac{3}{4}$?

  Ⓐ $3 \div 4$ Ⓒ $3 \div 40$

  Ⓑ $4 \div 3$ Ⓓ $4 \div 30$

Remember . . .

The fraction bar is another way of showing division.

$$\frac{a}{b} = a \div b$$

Step-By-Step

Use the fact that a fraction is another way of showing division to answer **example 7**.

1 Think: If 3 pies are shared equally by 4 people, how many pieces of pie does each person receive? Mark the circles to show your answer.

2 What fraction of a pie does each person receive?

3 Choose the division expression that represents this situation.

8 If 3 people share a 20-pound box of peanuts evenly, which is the best estimate of the number of pounds of peanuts each person will get?

Ⓐ between 4 and 5 pounds

Ⓑ between 5 and 6 pounds

Ⓒ between 6 and 7 pounds

Ⓓ between 7 and 8 pounds

8 Which expression has the same meaning as $\frac{5}{6}$?

Ⓐ $6 \div 5$

Ⓑ $60 \div 5$

Ⓒ $50 \div 6$

Ⓓ $5 \div 6$

Multiplying with Fractions and Mixed Numbers

9 A muffin recipe calls for $\frac{3}{4}$ cup of oil. If Troy makes 3 batches of muffins, how many cups of oil does he need?

Answer: _____ cups

Think It Through

For **example 8**, you can think of multiplication facts. 3 times 6 is 18 and 3 times 7 is 21, so 20 divided by 3 is between [ ] and [ ].

9 Leroy wrote $\frac{1}{2} + \frac{1}{2} = \frac{1}{4}$. Is his answer reasonable? Explain.

Answer: _____

Explanation: _____

Step-By-Step

Multiply $\frac{3}{4}$ cup by 3 to find the amount of oil for **example 9**.

1 Write the whole number as an improper fraction.

$$\frac{3}{4} \times \frac{3}{\boxed{}}$$

2 Multiply the numerators. Multiply the denominators.

$$\frac{3}{4} \times \frac{3}{1} = \frac{3 \times 3}{4 \times 1} = \frac{\boxed{}}{\boxed{}}$$

3 Write the fraction in simplest form.

$$\frac{9}{4} = 9 \div 4 = 2\frac{\boxed{}}{4}$$

GO ON

10 A rug will cover $\frac{3}{5}$ of the length and $\frac{3}{4}$ of the width of a room.

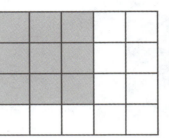

What fraction of the room will it cover?

Answer: _____

11 Maria needs $5\frac{3}{4}$ pounds of apples for each pitcher of apple juice she makes. How many pounds of apples does she need for 3 pitchers of juice?

Answer: _____ pounds

Step-By-Step

The area the rug in **exercise 10** covers can be found by multiplying $\frac{3}{5}$ times $\frac{3}{4}$.

1 Multiply the numerators. Multiply the denominators.

$$\frac{3}{5} \times \frac{3}{4} = \frac{3 \times 3}{5 \times 4} = \frac{}{}$$

2 Use the model to check. Are 9 out of 20 equal parts shaded?

Step-By-Step

You can multiply $5\frac{3}{4}$ pounds by 3 to find the number of pounds of apples Maria needs for **example 11**.

1 Write an equation. Let p be the number of pounds of apples Maria needs.

$$p = 5\frac{3}{4} \times 3$$

2 Write the mixed number and the whole number as improper fractions.

$$p = \frac{23}{4} \times \frac{}{1}$$

3 Multiply and write the answer in simplest form.

$$p = \frac{23}{4} \times \frac{3}{1} = \frac{69}{4} = 17\frac{}{} \text{ pounds}$$

12 Laura multiplied $\frac{5}{6}$ by some number. She got a product of $\frac{3}{4}$.

$$\frac{5}{6} \times n = \frac{3}{4}$$

Which statement is true?

Ⓐ Laura multiplied by a fraction.

Ⓑ Laura multiplied by 1.

Ⓒ Laura multiplied by a mixed number.

Ⓓ Laura multiplied by an improper fraction.

Step-By-Step

You can find the answer to **example 12** without calculating.

1 Compare the product to the factor you know.

Is $\frac{3}{4}$ less than, equal to, or greater than $\frac{5}{6}$?

2 Look at the *Multiplying Fractions* box on the next page. When the product is less than a factor, was it multiplied by a fraction, by 1, by a mixed number, or by an improper fraction?

Answer: _____

Try It

10 Alex had $\frac{3}{4}$ yard of copper wire. He used $\frac{1}{2}$ of the wire to hang a picture. What fraction of a yard did he use?

Ⓐ $\frac{2}{3}$ yd

Ⓑ $\frac{3}{4}$ yd

Ⓒ $\frac{1}{2}$ yd

Ⓓ $\frac{3}{8}$ yd

11 $\frac{1}{6} \times \frac{2}{3} \times \frac{9}{10} =$

Answer: _____

12 In this model, $\frac{2}{3}$ is striped and then $\frac{3}{4}$ of that area is shaded. What does the model show?

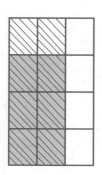

Ⓐ $\frac{3}{4} \times \frac{2}{3} = \frac{2}{6} = \frac{1}{3}$

Ⓑ $\frac{3}{4} \times \frac{2}{3} = \frac{6}{8} = \frac{3}{4}$

Ⓒ $\frac{3}{4} \times \frac{2}{3} = \frac{6}{12} = \frac{1}{2}$

Ⓓ $\frac{3}{4} \times \frac{2}{3} = \frac{8}{12} = \frac{2}{3}$

13 Dominic has $\frac{9}{10}$ meter of fancy leather. He uses $\frac{1}{3}$ of the leather to make a collar for his cat. How much leather is left?

Ⓐ $\frac{1}{3}$ m

Ⓑ $\frac{3}{5}$ m

Ⓒ $\frac{7}{10}$ m

Ⓓ $\frac{3}{10}$ m

14 Mindy drives at a speed of 40 miles per hour for $\frac{2}{5}$ of an hour. How far does she go?

Answer: _____

15 Latoya needs $2\frac{1}{2}$ cups of sugar for each batch of chocolate chip cookies. If she bakes 4 batches, how many cups of sugar will she need?

Ⓐ 5 cups

Ⓑ $7\frac{1}{2}$ cups

Ⓒ 10 cups

Ⓓ 12 cups

GO ON

Multiplying Fractions

When you multiply a number by a fraction, the product is less than the number.

$$5 \times \frac{2}{3} = \frac{5}{1} \times \frac{2}{3} = \frac{10}{3} = 3\frac{1}{3} \qquad \frac{2}{1} \times \frac{1}{3} = \frac{1}{6}$$

When you multiply a number by 1, the product is the same as the number.

$$5 \times 1 = 5 \qquad \frac{14}{15} \times \frac{1}{1} = \frac{14}{15}$$

When you multiply a number by an improper fraction or a mixed number, the product is greater than the number.

$$5 \times 1\frac{1}{2} = \frac{5}{1} \times \frac{3}{2} = \frac{15}{2} = 7\frac{1}{2}$$

Dividing with Fractions

13 If $\frac{1}{2}$ of a sheet of paper is divided into 4 equal pieces, what fraction of the sheet of paper will each piece be?

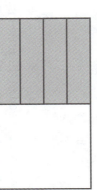

Answer: _____

Step-By-Step

To divide $\frac{1}{2}$ by 4 for **example 13**, you multiply by the **reciprocal** of 4.

1 Write an equation. Let f be the fraction of the sheet of paper.

$$f = \frac{1}{2} \div 4$$

2 Rewrite the division by 4 as a multiplication by the reciprocal of 4.

$$f = \frac{1}{2} \times \frac{1}{4}$$

3 Multiply.

$$f = \frac{1}{2} \times \frac{1}{4} = \frac{}{}$$

Reciprocals

$\frac{1}{8}$ and 8 are **reciprocals**. Their product is 1.

$$\frac{1}{8} \times \frac{8}{1} = \frac{8}{8} = 1$$

14 Kareem has 6 cups of orange juice. How many $\frac{1}{3}$-cup servings of orange juice can he make?

Ⓐ 2

Ⓑ 9

Ⓒ 18

Ⓓ 24

Step-By-Step

For example 14, divide 6 by $\frac{1}{3}$.

1 Write an equation. Let s be the number of servings.

$$s = 6 \div \frac{1}{3}$$

2 Rewrite the equation as a multiplication by the reciprocal of $\frac{1}{3}$.

$$s = 6 \times \boxed{}$$

3 Solve for s.

$$s = 6 \times 3 = \boxed{}$$

Try It

16 $\frac{3}{4} \div \frac{3}{8} =$

Ⓐ $\frac{3}{4} \times \frac{8}{3}$ Ⓒ $\frac{4}{3} \times \frac{8}{3}$

Ⓑ $\frac{1}{3} \times \frac{4}{8}$ Ⓓ $\frac{4}{3} \times \frac{3}{8}$

17 Which division equation is shown by this model?

$\frac{1}{2}$				$\frac{1}{2}$			
$\frac{1}{8}$	$\frac{1}{8}$	$\frac{1}{8}$	$\frac{1}{8}$	$\frac{1}{8}$	$\frac{1}{8}$	$\frac{1}{8}$	$\frac{1}{8}$

Ⓐ $\frac{1}{8} \div \frac{1}{4} = \frac{1}{2}$

Ⓑ $\frac{1}{8} \div \frac{1}{2} = 4$

Ⓒ $\frac{1}{2} \div \frac{1}{4} = \frac{1}{2}$

Ⓓ $\frac{1}{2} \div \frac{1}{8} = 4$

18 Rob has $\frac{15}{16}$ pound of chocolates. He divides it into 5 equal groups. How much does each group weigh?

Answer: _____

19 $\frac{8}{9} \div \frac{2}{3}$

Answer: _____

20 Carla finds that she can make a small pillow from $\frac{3}{8}$ yard of fabric. How many pillows can she make from $4\frac{1}{2}$ yards of fabric?

Answer: _____

15 **Part A:** Lily and Eden each have a candy bar. Their candy bars are the same size. Lily eats $\frac{2}{3}$ of her candy bar; Eden eats $\frac{3}{4}$ of hers. Who ate more—Lily or Eden?

Steps 1 & 2

Lily's Candy Bar

Eden's Candy Bar

I need to divide Lily's candy bar into

_____ equal pieces and Eden's into

_____ equal pieces.

Step 3

I shade _____ sections of Lily's candy bar

and _____ sections of Eden's candy bar.

Now I can compare and answer the question in Part A: Who ate more?

_____ ate more of her candy bar.

Step-By-Step

Plan how you will solve each step of the problem.

My Plan: *I will draw and label two equally sized candy bars. I will use my drawing to help me answer the questions. I will remember that when I need to convert fractions to a common denominator, I must find a number that is a multiple of both denominators.*

Part A

1 First, I'll need to draw two rectangles to represent the candy bars. I'll use my ruler to make sure they are the same size.

2 Next, I need to divide each candy bar into equal sections according to how each girl divided her own bar.

   The denominator tells me the number of sections. I use my ruler to do this so it is easier to compare the portions.

3 Now I shade in the amount that each girl ate. The numerator tells me how many sections to shade.

   Now I can compare and answer the question in Part A: Who ate more?

Unit 4 Application continued

Part B: What fraction of Lily's bar is uneaten? If you add the uneaten portion of Lily's candy bar to the part that she ate, does that amount represent one whole?

Step 4

_____ of Lily's candy bar is uneaten.

Step 5

$$\frac{}{\text{Fraction Lily ate}} + \frac{}{\substack{\text{Fraction} \\ \text{Lily didn't} \\ \text{eat}}} = \frac{}{}$$

Part B

4 Now I need to determine how much of Lily's candy bar remains. I can look at the diagram I drew in Part A to answer this question.

5 If I look at the diagram, I can see that the part that Lily ate plus the part that she didn't eat make up the whole candy bar.

So if I add the fraction Lily ate to the fraction she didn't eat, the answer will be 1, or the whole candy bar.

21 **Part A:** John has 4 sets of marbles. Each set contains 6 marbles. Write and solve a multiplication equation to show the total number of marbles John has.

Answer: _____

Part B: John gives one set of marbles to his friend Lisa. Write and solve a multiplication equation to show the total number of marbles John has left.

Answer: _____

Part C: John gives $\frac{1}{2}$ of a set to Chris. Write and solve a multiplication equation to show the total number of marbles John gives to Chris.

Answer: _____

Part D: Explain why Chris received fewer than 6 marbles.

Explanation: _____
_____
_____

22 **Part A:** Amanda has $\frac{1}{2}$ pound of cheese. She needs to divide this cheese into 6 equal portions. Write and solve an equation that illustrates this situation, using the variable x to represent the number of pounds of cheese in each share.

Answer: _____

Part B: Draw a diagram to represent the problem above, with a circle representing the whole pound of cheese. Label one of the 6 equal portions with the fraction of the whole it represents.

23 **Part A:** A rectangle has a length of $\frac{3}{10}$ of a cm and a width of $\frac{2}{10}$ of a cm. What is the total perimeter of the rectangle? Show your work below.

Answer: _____

Part B: What is the total area of the rectangle? Show your work below.

Answer: _____

Go for it!

Test Practice 4: Fractions

Estimated time: 30 minutes

Directions: Answer each question.

1 Adriana poured $\frac{1}{3}$ of a gallon of paint into a smaller container. Then she used $\frac{2}{5}$ of that amount to paint a door. What part of a gallon of paint did she use?

Ⓐ $\frac{1}{6}$ gal   Ⓒ $\frac{2}{5}$ gal

Ⓑ $\frac{5}{6}$ gal   Ⓓ $\frac{1}{5}$ gal

2 Vinnie is painting a barn. He did $\frac{3}{4}$ of the job last weekend and $\frac{1}{8}$ this morning. What fraction of the barn has Vinnie painted?

Ⓐ $\frac{1}{3}$ Ⓒ $\frac{3}{4}$

Ⓑ $\frac{2}{3}$ Ⓓ $\frac{7}{8}$

3 What is true about the product when 12 is multiplied by a mixed number?

Ⓐ The product is greater than 12.

Ⓑ The product is the reciprocal of the mixed number.

Ⓒ The product is less than 12.

Ⓓ The product is equal to the sum of 12 and the mixed number.

4 Payton has 4 bags of potting soil. She is going to put the same amount of the soil into each of 5 pots. What fraction of a bag of potting soil will she put in each pot? Show your work below.

Answer: _____

5 It is $\frac{7}{8}$ of a mile from Ja-Lisa's house to Margit's house. Ja-Lisa has walked $\frac{1}{4}$ mile on her way to Margit's house. How much farther does she have to go?

Ⓐ $\frac{3}{4}$ mi   Ⓒ $\frac{2}{3}$ mi

Ⓑ $\frac{5}{8}$ mi   Ⓓ $1\frac{1}{2}$ mi

6 How many $\frac{1}{2}$-inch long beads does Nora need to make a bracelet 6 inches long?

Answer: _____

7 Which shows another way to find the product of $32 \times \frac{1}{8}$?

Ⓐ $32 \div 8$ Ⓒ $32 - 8$

Ⓑ $\frac{1}{8} \div 32$ Ⓓ $8 \div 32$

8 Use this area model to help you find the product of $\frac{2}{5}$ and $\frac{1}{3}$.

$$\frac{2}{5} \times \frac{1}{3} =$$

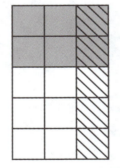

Answer: _____

9 Nadia peeled $5\frac{2}{3}$ pounds of potatoes. Robert peeled $4\frac{5}{12}$ pounds. How many more pounds of potatoes did Nadia peel than Robert?

Ⓐ $1\frac{1}{12}$ lb Ⓒ $1\frac{1}{4}$ lb

Ⓑ $1\frac{1}{3}$ lb Ⓓ $1\frac{1}{2}$ lb

10 Sergio drew this model.

What does it show?

Ⓐ $\frac{1}{3}$ of $\frac{1}{4}$ of a yard of fabric

Ⓑ $\frac{1}{4}$ of $\frac{1}{3}$ of a yard of fabric

Ⓒ $\frac{1}{3}$ of 4 yards of fabric

Ⓓ $\frac{1}{4}$ of 3 yards of fabric

11 Five friends are sharing 2 pizzas. If each person eats the same amount, what fraction of a pizza will each person eat?

Answer: _____

12 Teri walked $1\frac{3}{5}$ miles from home to school. After school she walked $2\frac{3}{10}$ miles to the park. How far did Teri walk altogether? Show your work below.

Answer: _____

13 What is the best estimate of the total weight of two books that weigh $\frac{5}{9}$ pound and $\frac{7}{8}$ pound?

Ⓐ $\frac{1}{2}$ pound Ⓒ $1\frac{1}{2}$ pounds

Ⓑ 1 pound Ⓓ 2 pounds

14 If 4 friends share a 25-pound bag of oranges, what is the best estimate of the number of pounds of oranges each will get?

Ⓐ between 3 pounds and 4 pounds

Ⓑ between 4 pounds and 5 pounds

Ⓒ between 5 pounds and 6 pounds

Ⓓ between 6 pounds and 7 pounds

15 Create a story for this equation and solve for m.

$$\frac{1}{2} \times \frac{4}{10} = m$$

Answer: _____

16 Jason added $\frac{1}{2} + \frac{2}{3} = \frac{3}{5}$. Is his answer reasonable? Explain why or why not.

Answer: _____

STOP

Points Earned/Total = _____ /16

Measurement and Data

MATH Unit 5

1 Converting Measurements [**5.MD.1**]
2 Solving Measurement Problems [**5.MD.1**]
3 Line Plots [**5.MD.2**]
4 Modeling Volume [**5.MD.3, 5.MD.4, 5.MD.5.a**]
5 Calculating Volume [**5.MD.5.b, 5.MD.5.c**]
Unit 5 Application [**5.MD.3a, 5.MD.3b, 3.MD.5b, 5.MD.5c**]

Directions: Answer each question.

Converting Measurements

1 Ralph needs $3\frac{1}{2}$ gallons of fruit punch for a party. How many quarts should he buy?

Ⓐ $\frac{3}{4}$ qt

Ⓑ 7 qt

Ⓒ 14 qt

Ⓓ 31 qt

Remember . . .

To change from a smaller unit like inches to a larger unit like feet, divide.

smaller to larger $\div$

To change from a larger unit like gallons to a smaller unit like cups, multiply.

larger to smaller $\times$

Step-By-Step

Use the *Table of Common Measurements* to answer **example 1.**

1 Find the conversion equation for gallons to quarts.

$$1 \text{ gallon} = 4 \text{ quarts}$$

2 Multiply $3\frac{1}{2}$ by 4. Change the **mixed number** to an **improper fraction** before multiplying.

$$3\frac{1}{2} \times 4 = \frac{7}{2} \times 4 = \boxed{}$$

Table of Common Measurements

1 minute (min) = 60 seconds (sec)	1 pound (lb) = 16 ounces (oz)
1 hour (hr) = 60 minutes (min)	1 ton (T) = 2,000 pounds (lb)
1 day (d) = 24 hours (hr)	1 cup (c) = 8 fluid ounces (fl oz)
1 week (wk) = 7 days (d)	1 pint (pt) = 2 cups (c)
1 year = 365 days (d)	1 quart (qt) = 2 pints (pt)
= 52 weeks (wk)	1 gallon (gal) = 4 quarts (qt)
= 12 months (mo)	
	1 centimeter (cm) = 10 millimeters (mm)
	1 meter (m) = 100 centimeters (cm)
1 foot (ft) = 12 inches (in.)	1 kilometer (km) = 1,000 meters (m)
1 yard (yd) = 36 inches (in.)	1 gram (g) = 1,000 milligrams (mg)
= 3 feet (ft)	1 kilogram (kg) = 1,000 grams (g)
1 mile (mi) = 5,280 feet (ft)	1 metric ton (t) = 1,000 kilograms (kg)
	1 liter (L) = 1,000 milliliters (mL)
	= 1,000 cubic centimeters (cm³)

Converting Measurements

2 Antonio's new kitten weighs 950 grams. What is the kitten's weight in kilograms?

Ⓐ 0.95 kg   Ⓒ 9,500 kg

Ⓑ 9.5 kg   Ⓓ 950,000 kg

Step-By-Step

In **example 2**, you must convert from a smaller unit of measurement to a larger unit.

1 Write the conversion equation for kilograms and grams.

$$1 \text{ kilogram} = \boxed{} \text{ grams}$$

2 Divide 950 by 1,000 to find the weight of the kitten in kilograms.

$$950 \text{ g} \div 1{,}000 = \boxed{} \text{ kg}$$

Converting Between Metric Units

Metric units are based on a decimal system. You can convert between units by moving the decimal point.

1 kilometer = 1,000 meters

5.6 kilometers = 5.600 km = 5,600 meters

1 meter = 0.001 kilometers

5.6 meters = 005.6 m = 0.0056 kilometers

GO ON

3 Omar's thermos holds 2 pints of liquid. Rosa's holds 3 cups. Which describes the capacities of the two thermoses?

Ⓐ They hold the same amount.

Ⓑ Omar's thermos holds half as much.

Ⓒ Rosa's thermos holds more.

Ⓓ Omar's thermos holds more.

Think It Through

To compare the thermoses in **example 3**, convert the measurements to the same unit. Since cups are the smaller unit, convert 2 pints to cups and compare the capacities.

1 pint = 2 cups

2 pints = ☐ cups

4 cups is more than 3 cups, so Omar's thermos holds more.

Try It

1 Norm's cat weighs 5.5 kilograms. What is the cat's weight in grams? Explain or show how you got your answer.

Answer: _____

2 Rosa's bedroom is 120 inches wide. How wide is her bedroom in feet? Show your work below.

Answer: _____

Solving Measurement Problems

4 Alex needs 1 liter of broth for a soup recipe. He has 750 milliliters of broth. How much more broth does he need?

Answer: _____

Step-By-Step

To find how much more broth Alex needs in **example 4**, you need to set up a subtraction problem.

1 Convert liters to milliliters.

$$1 \text{ L} = 1{,}000 \text{ mL}$$

2 Subtract the amount he has, 750 mL, from the amount he needs, 1,000 mL.

$$1{,}000 \text{ mL} - 750 \text{ mL} = \boxed{} \text{ mL}$$

5 Janeka needs one piece of pipe 5 feet 8 inches long and another 2 feet 6 inches long. How much pipe does Janeka need in all?

Ⓐ 3 ft 3 in.   Ⓒ 7 ft 4 in.

Ⓑ 7 ft 2 in.   Ⓓ 8 ft 2 in.

Step-By-Step

Follow these steps to find the total length of pipe that Janeka needs in **example 5**.

1 Stack the measures to make it easier to calculate.

$$\begin{array}{r} 5 \text{ ft } 8 \text{ in.} \\ + \; 2 \text{ ft } 6 \text{ in.} \\ \hline \end{array}$$

2 Add the inches first. Notice that the number of inches is greater than 12. Convert 14 inches into feet and inches. Record the inches and carry the feet.

$$\begin{array}{r} 1 \\ 5 \text{ ft } 8 \text{ in.} \\ + \; 2 \text{ ft } 6 \text{ in.} \\ \hline \boxed{} \;\; 2 \text{ in.} \end{array}$$

3 Add the feet, including the amount carried.

GO ON ↑

6 Myra made this line plot of the weights of some oranges she picked from her tree.

Orange Weights

	X		
X	X	X	
X	X	X	X
X	X	X	X
$\frac{1}{8}$	$\frac{1}{4}$	$\frac{3}{8}$	$\frac{1}{2}$

Weight (in pounds)

Myra puts all of the oranges that weigh $\frac{1}{4}$ pound or less into one bag. She puts all of the oranges that weigh more than $\frac{1}{4}$ pound in another bag.

Which bag weighs more? _____

Step-By-Step

For **example 6** find the total weight for oranges that weigh $\frac{1}{8}$ and $\frac{1}{4}$ pound. Then find the total weight of oranges that weigh $\frac{3}{8}$ and $\frac{1}{2}$ pound.

1 There are 4 Xs above $\frac{1}{8}$. There are 5 Xs above $\frac{1}{4}$. Multiply to find the total for each weight. Add to find the total for the two weights.

$$\left(4 \times \frac{1}{8}\right) + \left(5 \times \frac{1}{4}\right) = \frac{4}{8} + \frac{5}{4}$$
$$= \frac{2}{4} + \frac{5}{4} = \frac{7}{4} = 1\frac{}{4}$$

2 There are 3 Xs above $\frac{3}{8}$ and 2 Xs above $\frac{1}{2}$. Multiply and add to find the total weight of oranges that weigh more than $\frac{1}{4}$ pound.

$$\left(3 \times \frac{3}{8}\right) + \left(2 \times \frac{1}{2}\right) = \frac{9}{8} + \frac{2}{2}$$
$$= 1\frac{1}{8} + 1 =$$

3 Compare the two weights.

$$1\frac{3}{4} \qquad 2\frac{1}{8}$$

Making a Line Plot

1 Identify the greatest and least numbers in your data.

2 Select and draw a scale that includes all of the data.

3 Label the scale.

4 Draw an X to plot each number in your data.

5 Label the graph.

3 Juanita has a board 4 feet 8 inches long. If she cuts off a piece 2 feet 6 inches long, how long will the remaining piece be?

Ⓐ 7 ft 2 in.

Ⓑ 3 ft 2 in.

Ⓒ 2 ft 2 in.

Ⓓ 2 ft 4 in.

4 Carlos is building a desk. He needs one piece of wood 3 feet 6 inches long and another piece 2 feet 6 inches long. How much wood does Carlos need?

Ⓐ 5 feet

Ⓑ 6 feet

Ⓒ 6 feet 6 inches

Ⓓ 7 feet

Modeling Volume

7 This rectangular prism is built with 1-inch cubes. What is the volume?

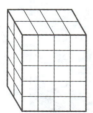

Ⓐ 10 in.³

Ⓑ 20 in.³

Ⓒ 40 in.³

Ⓓ 80 in.³

Step-By-Step

For **example 7**, recall that the volume of a figure is the amount of space inside it.

1 Find the number of cubes in one layer.

$5 \times 2 =$ ☐ cubic inches

2 Multiply by the number of layers.

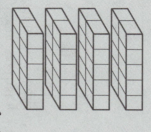

$4 \times 10 =$ ☐ cubic inches

Unit Cubes

The length, width, and height of a cube are all the same. A cube that is 1 unit long, 1 unit wide, and 1 unit tall is a **unit cube**. Its volume is 1 cubic unit.

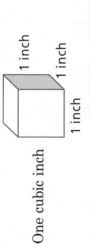

One cubic inch

1 inch

1 inch

1 inch

GO ON

8 José is packing centimeter cubes into this box. If he fills the box without leaving any gaps, how many centimeter cubes can he put in the box?

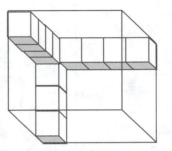

Answer: _____ cubic centimeters

Step-By-Step

For **example 8**, count to find how many cubes long, cubes wide, and cubes tall the box is.

1 Multiply the number of cubes along the length by the number of cubes along the width to find the number of cubes on the bottom layer.

$5 \times 4 =$ ▭

2 Multiply the number of cubes in the bottom layer by the number of layers to find the total number of cubes the box will hold. This is the volume of the box.

$20 \times 5 =$ ▭

Calculating Volume

9 The area of Aman's living room floor is 320 square feet. The living room is a rectangular prism that is 12 feet in height. What is the volume of the living room?

Answer: _____

Think It Through

Multiply the area of the living room floor times the height of the room to find the volume for **example 9.**

Volume = 320×12

Volume = ▭

Volume = ▭ cubic feet

Volume of a Rectangular Prism

The volume of a rectangular prism can be found by multiplying its length times its width times its height.

$$V = l \times w \times h$$

If you know the area of the base, the volume can be found by multiplying the base times the height.

$$V = b \times h$$

Calculating Volume

10 Nichole built a shed for her lawn tractor next to her garage.

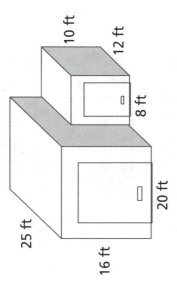

25 ft
10 ft
12 ft
8 ft
16 ft
20 ft

What is the total volume of the two buildings?

Answer: _____

Step-By-Step

Use the formula $V = l \times w \times h$ to find the volume of each building in **example 10**.

1 Read the diagram and substitute numbers into the formula to find the volume of the garage.

$$V = l \times w \times h$$

$$V = 25 \times 20 \times 16$$

$$V = \boxed{} \text{ cubic feet}$$

2 Find the volume of the shed.

$$V = l \times w \times h$$

$$V = 12 \times 8 \times 10$$

$$V = \boxed{} \text{ cubic feet}$$

3 Add to find the total volume. Remember to include units.

$$8,000 + 960 = \boxed{} \text{ cubic feet}$$

Try It

5 How many cubic units are there in the volume of this rectangular prism? Show your work below.

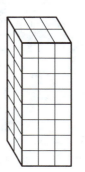

Answer:

6 Which expression equals the volume of a cube with edges that are 5 units long?

5
5
5

Ⓐ 5×5 Ⓒ $5 + 5 + 5$

Ⓑ $6 \times (5 \times 5)$ Ⓓ $5 \times 5 \times 5$

GO ON

7 How many cubic feet of soil are needed to fill this flower planter?

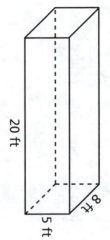

20 ft

8 ft

5 ft

Ⓐ 33 ft³   Ⓒ 260 ft³

Ⓑ 200 ft³   Ⓓ 800 ft³

8 Trudy's living room is 20 feet long, 15 feet wide, and 10 feet tall. Find the area of the floor and the volume of the room. Write each answer on the proper line below.

_____ square feet

_____ cubic feet

9 A factory packs chairs in cartons that are 1-meter cubes. How much volume is taken up by 200 of these cartons?

Ⓐ 200 m³

Ⓑ 600 m³

Ⓒ 40,000 m³

Ⓓ 8,000,000 m³

10 How much dirt must be removed to dig a hole that is 4 feet long, 3 feet wide, and 2 feet deep?

Ⓐ 9 ft³

Ⓑ 24 ft³

Ⓒ 48 ft³

Ⓓ 52 ft³

11 How many cubic inches of plastic peanuts are needed to fill this carton halfway full?

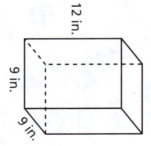

12 in.

9 in.

9 in.

Answer: _____

12 What is the volume of the prism that can be made from this pattern? Show your work below.

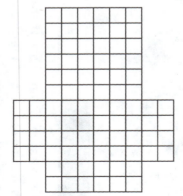

Answer: _____

11 **Part A:** Brian is packing to move. The
moving truck can hold a total of 1,008
cubic feet. If the truck is 14 feet long
and 9 feet high, how many feet wide is
it?

14 feet

8 feet

Step-By-Step

Plan how you will solve each step of the
problem.

Part A

1 I need to use the formula for the volume
of a rectangle to solve this part of the
problem. $V = l \times w \times h$

I will fill in the what I know: volume,
length, and height.

Then I can use that information to
calculate the missing measurement, or the
width. I'll remember to label my answer
with the correct units.

Step 1

_____ = _____ × _____ × _____
volume   length   width   height

I need to figure out the width, or what
number, when multiplied by the given
length and the height of the truck,
results in a volume measurement of
1,008 cubic feet. The width is _____.

Answer: _____

GO ON

Part B: Brian has packed boxes he wants to put in the truck. Each box is $2\frac{1}{2}$ feet high, 2 feet wide, and 2 feet long. What is the volume of the packed boxes?

Step 2

Answer: _____

$$\underline{\hspace{2cm}} \times \underline{\hspace{2cm}} \times \underline{\hspace{2cm}} = \underline{\hspace{2cm}}$$
length   width   height   volume

Part C: What is the maximum number of boxes that will fit in the truck? Explain your answer with words or a diagram.

Step 3

$$\frac{\underline{\hspace{2cm}}}{\text{total volume of the truck}} \div \frac{\underline{\hspace{2cm}}}{\text{volume of one box}} = \frac{\underline{\hspace{2cm}}}{\text{maximum number of boxes that will fit}}$$

Answer: _____

Step 4

Explanation: _____
_____
_____
_____

Part B

2 Now I need to find the volume of a single moving box. I know the formula is $V = l \times w \times h$ and I know all three measurements.

I substitute the measurements into the formula and solve for the volume. I remember to label my answer with the correct units.

Part C

3 I will compare the total volume of the moving truck against the volume of a single box to determine the maximum number that will fit in the truck.

I know the volume of 1 box and the total volume of the truck. In order to determine the maximum number of boxes that will fit, I need to divide.

4 I'll explain my answer in writing or with a diagram.

13 **Part A:** Amanda completely fills three bottles with water. She pours 500 mL into each bottle. How many mL did she pour in total?

Answer: _____

Part B: How many liters does she use in total?

Answer: _____

Part C: How many liters are in each bottle?

Answer: _____

14 **Part A:** A rectangular prism has a total volume of 20 cubic inches. What are the possible dimensions of the prism?

Answer: _____

Part B: Darius says that the prism is 10 inches long, 2 inches wide, and 8 inches high. Is this a possible answer? Why or why not?

Answer: _____

Explanation: _____

_____

_____

15 **Part A:** A rectangular prism has a length of 2 feet, a width of 1 foot, and a height of 3 feet. What is the volume of this prism in cubic feet? Show your work.

Answer: _____

Part B: What is the volume of the prism in Part A in cubic inches? Show your work.

Answer: _____

Part C: What is the volume of the prism in Part A in cubic yards? Show your work.

Answer: _____

Test Practice 5: Measurement and Data

Estimated time: 20 minutes

Directions: Answer each question.

1 Jelan practiced the bagpipes for 3 hours. How many minutes did she practice?

- Ⓐ 24 minutes
- Ⓑ 60 minutes
- Ⓒ 120 minutes
- Ⓓ 180 minutes

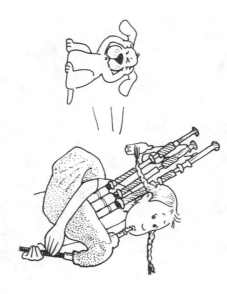

2 Gayle bought 4.3 kilograms of fancy nuts. How can she determine how many grams she bought?

- Ⓐ multiply by 100
- Ⓑ multiply by 1,000
- Ⓒ divide by 100
- Ⓓ divide by 1,000

3 How many small cubes would it take to build the big cube?

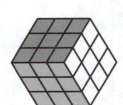

- Ⓐ 3 small cubes
- Ⓑ 9 small cubes
- Ⓒ 18 small cubes
- Ⓓ 27 small cubes

Answer: _____

Archie made the line plot to show the time he spent at each of 9 basketball practices. Use the line plot for questions 4 and 5.

Time Spent at Basketball Practice

	X			
X	X	X	X	X
X	X	X	X	X
$1\frac{1}{2}$	$1\frac{3}{4}$	2	$2\frac{1}{4}$	$2\frac{1}{2}$

Time (in hours)

4 If the total time spent at practice stayed the same but all practices were the same length, how long would each practice have lasted?

Answer: _____

5 How much longer did Archie spend at the longest 3 practices than he spent at the 3 two-hour practices?

Answer: _____

6 What is the volume of this rectangular prism?

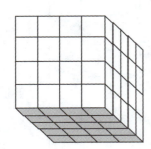

Answer: _____

7 How many cubic feet of soil are needed to fill this flower planter? (Hint: Use the formula $V = l \times w \times h$.)

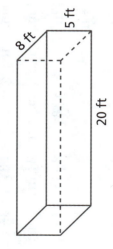

8 ft

20 ft

5 ft

Ⓐ 33 ft³   Ⓒ 260 ft³

Ⓑ 200 ft³   Ⓓ 800 ft³

8 Sid combined 6 quarts of cranberry juice with 1 gallon of lemonade to make punch for a family reunion. How many quarts of punch did he make in all?

Ⓐ 6 quarts

Ⓑ 7 quarts

Ⓒ 8 quarts

Ⓓ 10 quarts

9 Ramiro's house is 12 yards long. How many feet long is his house?

Ⓐ 4 ft   Ⓒ 36 ft

Ⓑ 15 ft   Ⓓ 40 ft

10 How many milliliters of tea does a 2-liter pot hold?

Ⓐ 20,000 mL

Ⓑ 2,000 mL

Ⓒ 200 mL

Ⓓ 20 mL

11 Jovan's bookcase is wider on the bottom than on the top.

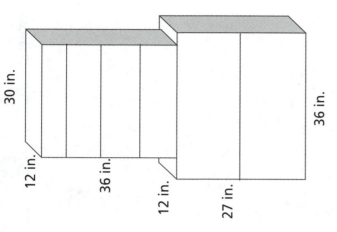

30 in.

12 in.

36 in.

12 in.

27 in.

36 in.

What is the total volume of the bookcase?

Answer: _____

12 Paolo bought 2 melons. One weighed 6 pounds 13 ounces, and the other weighed 5 pounds 11 ounces. What is the total weight of the melons?

Answer: _____

13 Roger is 6 feet tall. Perry is 77 inches tall. How much taller than Roger is Perry?

Ⓐ 71 inches

Ⓑ 17 inches

Ⓒ 7 inches

Ⓓ 5 inches

14 A squash weighs 42 ounces. What is its weight in pounds and ounces? Show your work below.

Answer: _____

15 William measured the diameters of stones he gathered.

4 in., 3 in., $2\frac{3}{4}$ in., $2\frac{3}{4}$ in., $3\frac{1}{4}$ in., $3\frac{1}{2}$ in.,
3 in., 3 in., $3\frac{1}{2}$ in., 4 in., $2\frac{3}{4}$ in., $3\frac{1}{4}$ in.,
4 in., 4 in., 3 in., $3\frac{1}{4}$ in., $3\frac{1}{4}$ in., 4 in., 3 in.,
$2\frac{3}{4}$ in.

Make a line plot of the diameters. Then use the line plot to answer the question.

If William lines all of the 3-inch stones up in one row and all of the $3\frac{1}{4}$-inch stones up in another row, how will the lengths of the two rows compare?

Answer: _____

Points Earned/Total = _____ /15

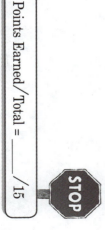
STOP

MATH
Unit
6

Geometry

1 The Coordinate System [5.G.1, 5.G.2]

2 Graphing Patterns [5.G.1, 5.G.2, 5.OA.3]

3 Graphing Geometric Figures [5.G.1, 5.G.2]

4 Properties of Quadrilaterals [5.G.3]

5 Classifying Quadrilaterals [5.G.3, 5.G.4]

Unit 6 Application [5.G.1, 5.G.2, 5.G.3]

Directions: Answer each question.

The Coordinate System

Use this coordinate grid for examples 1 and 2.

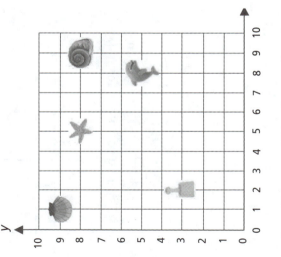

1 Gretchen drew a grid in the sand and buried sand toys for her brother to find. What ordered pair gives the location of the dolphin toy?

Answer:

Ordered Pairs

An **ordered pair** is made up of an *x*-coordinate and a *y*-coordinate. The point (0, 0) has *x*-coordinate 0 and *y*-coordinate 0. It is called the **origin**.

Step-By-Step

For **example 1**, the first number in an **ordered pair** tells you the horizontal location on the coordinate grid. The second number tells you the vertical location.

1 Find the dolphin. Trace right on the horizontal axis until the dolphin is directly above. The number on the *x*-axis is the first number in the ordered pair. It is called the *x*-coordinate. (8,)

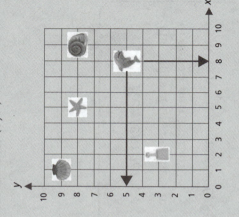

2 Trace up to the dolphin. Then trace across to the vertical axis. The number on the *y*-axis is the second number in the ordered pair. It is called the *y*-coordinate. (8, ☐)

GO ON

2 In the coordinate grid below, what toy is located at point (5, 8)?

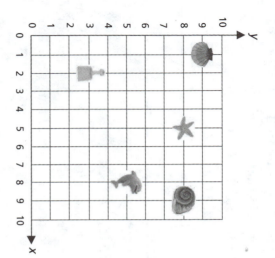

Ⓐ snail

Ⓑ shell

Ⓒ shovel

Ⓓ starfish

Think It Through

For **example 2**, start at 0. The first number in the ordered pair (5, 8) tells you to move 5 units right along the x-axis. The second number tells you to move 8 units up.

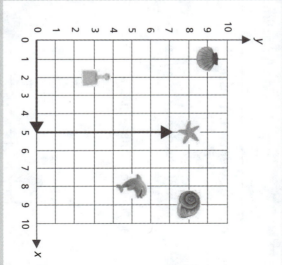

What toy is located 5 units right and 8 units up? _____

Remember . . .

The order of the numbers in an **ordered pair** matters.

(8, 5) is not the same as (5, 8).

Graphing Patterns

3 Beverly used corresponding terms from two patterns to make ordered pairs.

Add 5: 0, 5, 10, 15, 20, 25,... →

Add 10: 0, 10, 20, 30, 40, 50,... →

(0, 0), (5, 10), (10, 20), (15, 30), (20, 40), (25, 50)

Graph the ordered pairs on a coordinate grid.

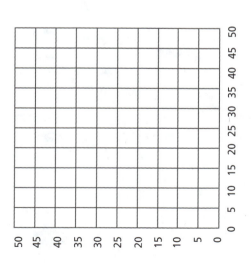

Describe the pattern shown by the points.

Answer: _____

Think It Through

For **example 3**, graph the ordered pairs and look for a pattern.

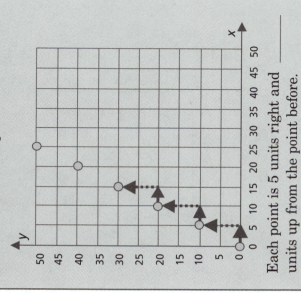

Each point is 5 units right and ___ units up from the point before.

GO ON

1 Which ordered pair gives the location of the square shown on this coordinate grid?

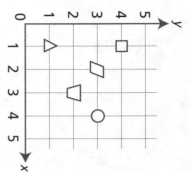

Ⓐ (1, 4)　　Ⓒ (4, 5)

Ⓑ (4, 1)　　Ⓓ (3, 2)

2 Which of the points shown on the coordinate grid is located at (2, 8)?

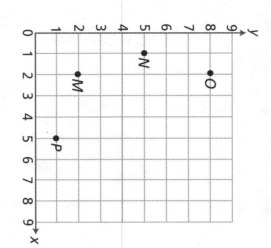

Ⓐ M　　Ⓒ O

Ⓑ N　　Ⓓ P

3 Which ordered pair gives the location of Point A?

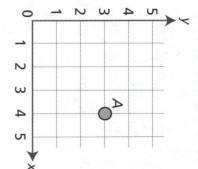

Ⓐ (4, 3)　　Ⓒ (3, 3)

Ⓑ (3, 4)　　Ⓓ (4, 4)

Open-Ended Practice

Some tests include questions in which you must explain how you solved a problem. You may also be asked to show your work, draw graphs, or make diagrams. The example below will give you practice responding to such questions.

Graphing Geometric Figures

4 Cecilia is drawing parallelogram ABCD on the coordinate grid below. She plotted and labeled points A, B, and C.

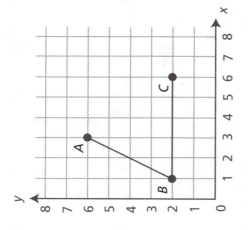

Part A

Plot and label point D so parallelogram ABCD is formed.

Part B

What is the ordered pair for point D?

Answer: _____

Math Tip

All horizontal lines are parallel to each other.

Step-By-Step

Be sure to answer all parts of open-ended questions. Also, be sure to show and label your work clearly. To answer the questions, follow these steps.

1 Opposite sides of a parallelogram are parallel and the same length. $\overline{BC}$ is a horizontal line. The side opposite $\overline{BC}$ will need to be horizontal and the same length.

2 To find the length of $\overline{BC}$, count units from one endpoint to the other. What is the length of $\overline{BC}$?

☐ units

3 To plot point D, start at point A. Count 5 units to the right along the horizontal grid line. Put a dot at that location and label it clearly with the letter D.

4 To find the first number of the ordered pair for point D, start at 0 and count the units to the right until you are directly below point D. How many units to the right of 0 is point D?

☐ units

To find the second number, count up until you reach point D.

☐ units up from 0

5 The ordered pair for point D is

(☐ , ☐).

GO ON

4   Plot the following points on the grid.

(2, −3), (2, 3), (0, −1)

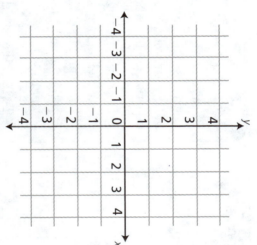

Then connect the points in the order given. Name the figure.

Answer: _____

5   Plot the following points on the grid below. Connect the points to create a closed figure.

(−1, 1), (4, 1), (4, 3), and (−1, 3)

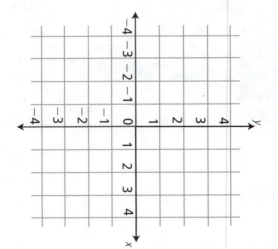

What kind of figure is it?

Answer: _____

Properties of Quadrilaterals

5 Wesley drew a quadrilateral with opposite sides parallel. All sides of the quadrilateral are the same length and none of the angles are right angles. What type of quadrilateral did Wesley draw?

Ⓐ square
Ⓑ rectangle
Ⓒ rhombus
Ⓓ trapezoid

Step-By-Step

Analyze to solve **example 5.**

1 Which of the quadrilaterals listed have opposite sides parallel?

2 Of those quadrilaterals, which have all sides the same length?

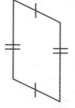

3 Of those quadrilaterals, which does not have any right angles?

Quadrilaterals

Parallelogram

- Opposite angles are equal.
- Opposite sides are the same length.
- Opposite sides are parallel.

Trapezoid

- Has only one pair of opposite sides parallel.

Rhombus

- Opposite angles are equal.
- All sides are the same length.
- Opposite sides are parallel.

Kite

- Has two pairs of adjacent same-length sides.

Square

- Has all right angles.
- All sides are the same length.
- Opposite sides are parallel.

Rectangle

- Has all right angles.
- Opposite sides are the same length.
- Opposite sides are parallel.

GO ON

6 Which term could **NOT** be used to describe the figure shown below?

Ⓐ polygon

Ⓑ quadrilateral

Ⓒ parallelogram

Ⓓ kite

Remember . . .

Dimensions that have the same markings have the same measure.

7 Which shape is **NOT** a parallelogram?

Ⓐ rectangle

Ⓑ rhombus

Ⓒ square

Ⓓ kite

Step-By-Step

The shape in **example 6** has four right angles and opposite sides the same length. Compare these properties to the properties of each answer.

1 A polygon is a many-sided figure.

Is the shape a polygon? ____

2 A quadrilateral has 4 sides.

Is the shape a quadrilateral? ____

3 A parallelogram has opposite sides the same length, opposite angles equal, and opposite sides parallel.

Is the shape a parallelogram? ____

4 A kite has two pairs of adjacent sides that are the same length.

Is the shape a kite? ____

5 Select the answer that does **NOT** name the shape.

Think It Through

For **example 7**, remember the properties of a parallelogram.

• Opposite sides are parallel.

• Opposite sides are the same length.

• Opposite angles are equal.

Which of the shapes given as an answer does not have these properties?

Properties of Quadrilaterals

8 Which statement is true?

Ⓐ All quadrilaterals are parallelograms.

Ⓑ All rhombi are rectangles.

Ⓒ All rectangles are squares.

Ⓓ All squares are rhombi.

Quadrilateral Relationships

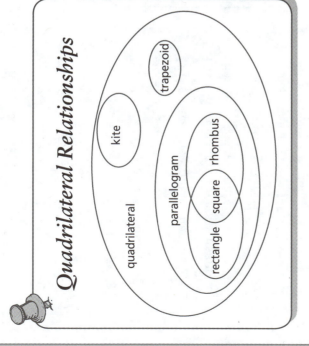

Step-By-Step

Use the Quadrilateral Relationships box below to help you see the relationships among the shapes for **example 8**. Think of the properties of each shape.

1 For answer A, do all shapes with 4 sides (quadrilaterals) have opposite sides parallel and the same length (parallelograms)?

Answer: _____

2 For answer B, do all quadrilaterals with 4 equal sides and opposite sides parallel (rhombi) also have 4 right angles (rectangles)?

Answer: _____

3 For answer C, do all quadrilaterals with opposite sides equal and 4 right angles (rectangles) also have 4 sides the same length (squares)?

Answer: _____

4 For answer D, do all quadrilaterals with 4 equal sides and 4 right angles (squares) also have 2 pairs of parallel sides (rhombi)?

Answer: _____

5 Choose the letter of the statement to which you answered *yes*.

GO ON

9 Classify this figure.

Ⓐ quadrilateral, parallelogram, rhombus

Ⓑ quadrilateral, parallelogram, rectangle

Ⓒ quadrilateral, parallelogram, rhombus, square

Ⓓ quadrilateral, parallelogram, rectangle, rhombus, square

Classification Path

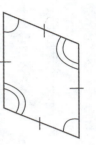

Polygons → quadrilaterals

quadrilaterals → parallelogram, trapezoid, kites

parallelogram → rectangle, rhombus

rectangle, rhombus → square

Step-By-Step

To classify the quadrilateral in **example 9**, list all of the names that apply to it. Use the diagram and the questions below to help you.

1 If a figure has four sides, it is a quadrilateral.

Is the figure a quadrilateral? _____

2 If a quadrilateral has 2 pairs of parallel sides, it is a parallelogram.

Is the quadrilateral a parallelogram. _____

3 If a parallelogram has 4 right angles, it is a rectangle.

Is the quadrilateral a parallelogram? _____

4 If a parallelogram has 4 equal length sides, it is a rhombus.

Is the parallelogram a rectangle? _____

5 If a figure is both a rectangle and a rhombus, it is a square.

Is the parallelogram a rhombus? _____

Is the figure a square? _____

6 Choose the answer that includes all of the names that apply. The last name is the most precise name for the quadrilateral.

Try It

6 Identify this quadrilateral.

Answer: _____

7 Classify this quadrilateral.

Ⓐ quadrilateral, parallelogram, rectangle, rhombus, square

Ⓑ quadrilateral, kite, rectangle, rhombus, square

Ⓒ trapezoid, rhombus, square

Ⓓ kite, rhombus, square

88 Geometry

Go for it!

10 **Part A:** Draw a set of perpendicular lines. Label the point at which the lines intersect with the number 0. Use your ruler to create identical scales on both the *x*- and *y*-axis, starting with 0 and counting by 1's up to 10.

Steps 1 & 2

Part B: Using the coordinate plane you just created, plot points at the following coordinates: (3, 0); (3, 3); (6, 3); (6, 0). Connect your points in the order listed.

Part C: Classify the shape you created. Justify your classification(s) using the definitions of the polygon(s) you identified.

Step 3

Answer: _____

_____

Step-By-Step

Plan how you will solve each step of the problem.

Part A

1 I know what it means for a pair of lines to be perpendicular. I draw my lines using that definition and label the indicated point. I use my ruler to create equally spaced scales on both axes that number from 0 to 10, counting by 1's.

Part B

2 In Part B, I need to plot the given points. I remember that the first coordinate listed in each pair corresponds to the *x*-axis.

I will plot all four sets of coordinates and then connect them in order.

Part C

3 Part C asks me to classify the shape I created by plotting the given points. I can use the classification path and definitions listed in this text to help me answer this question.

When I classify a shape, I include all the names that apply. The last name is the most precise name for the quadrilateral.

8 **Part A:** Use the given coordinate plane to draw a rectangle.

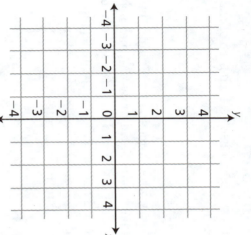

Part B: List the coordinates of your rectangle's vertices.

Answer: _____

Part C: Is your rectangle also a quadrilateral? Why or why not?

Answer: _____

9 **Part A:** Using your ruler and protractor, draw and label both a square and a rhombus.

Part B: Are all squares rhombuses? Why or why not?

Answer: _____

Part C: Are all rhombuses squares? Why or why not?

Answer: _____

Part D: Which classification includes more shapes: square or rhombus? Explain.

Answer: _____

10 **Part A:** Using the following Venn diagram, label the left area "Rectangle" and the right area "Rhombus."

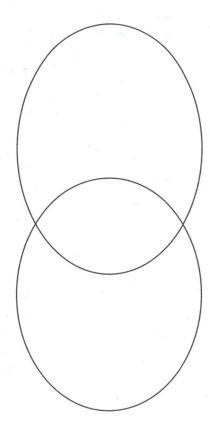

Part B: Of the two shapes, rectangle or rhombus, which must have right angles? Write the words "right angles" in the appropriate area.

Part C: Of the two shapes, which must have sides of equal length? Write the words "equal sides" where it belongs in the diagram.

Part D: Of the two shapes, which has four sides? Write "four sides" where it belongs in the diagram.

11 Name a quadrilateral that is not a parallelogram. Explain your answer using either words or a drawing.

Answer: _____

Explanation: _____

_____

_____

Test Practice 6: Geometry

Directions: Answer each question.

1 Which describes how to move from the origin on a coordinate grid to point (7, 3)?

Ⓐ Move 7 units up and 3 units right.

Ⓑ Move 7 units right and 3 units up.

Ⓒ Move 3 units up and 3 units right.

Ⓓ Move 7 units right and 7 units up.

2 Which of the following statements is NOT true?

Ⓐ A square has all right angles.

Ⓑ A trapezoid has two pairs of parallel sides.

Ⓒ A rhombus has 4 equal sides.

Ⓓ Opposite angles of a parallelogram are equal.

3 Which statement is NOT true?

Ⓐ All squares are rectangles.

Ⓑ All trapezoids are quadrilaterals.

Ⓒ All rhombuses are parallelograms.

Ⓓ All rectangles have acute angles.

4 Which quadrilateral is NOT a parallelogram?

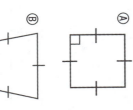
Ⓐ

Ⓒ

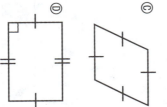
Ⓑ

Ⓓ

5 Cierra plotted 2 points and drew 1 side of a square.

y
10
9
8
7
6
5
4
3
2
1
0 1 2 3 4 5 6 7 8 9 10 x

Which 2 points can she plot for the other vertices of the square?

Ⓐ (3, 8) and (8, 8)

Ⓑ (8, 3) and (8, 8)

Ⓒ (3, 3) and (3, 8)

Ⓓ (3, 3) and (8, 3)

6 Classify this quadrilateral.

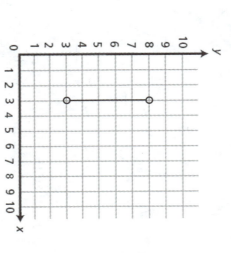

Ⓐ trapezoid

Ⓑ quadrilateral

Ⓒ rectangle

Ⓓ kite

Ernesto drew a coordinate grid and plotted the locations of items in his backyard. Use this coordinate grid for questions 7 and 8.

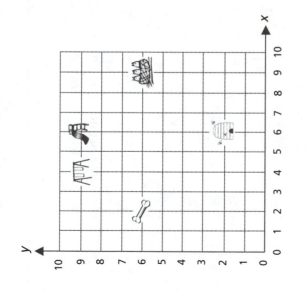

7 What item is located at point (9, 6)?

Ⓐ slide

Ⓑ bird's nest

Ⓒ bone

Ⓓ beehive

8 At what point is the swing located?

Answer: _____

9 Classify this figure.

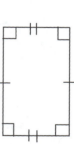

Ⓐ quadrilateral, parallelogram, rectangle

Ⓑ trapezoid, parallelogram, rectangle, square

Ⓒ parallelogram, rectangle, rhombus, square

Ⓓ parallelogram, rhombus, square

10 Plot the points (2, 3), (7, 3), (7, 6), and (4, 6) and connect them in order.

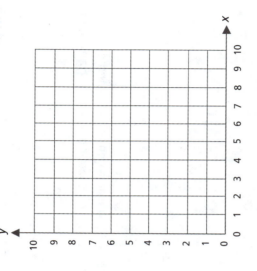

What quadrilateral did you draw?

Answer: _____

11 Suzanne started at 0 and wrote sequences for the rules *Add 3* and *Add 6*. She used corresponding terms from the patterns to make ordered pairs. Which point is one of the ordered pairs?

Ⓐ (6, 3)

Ⓑ (0, 6)

Ⓒ (6, 9)

Ⓓ (9, 18)

12 Is a rhombus always a parallelogram? Explain why or why not.

Answer: _____

13 List the quadrilaterals that have at least 1 pair of parallel sides.

Answer: _____

14 Start at 20. Write sequences for the rules *Subtract 3* and *Subtract 2*. Use corresponding terms from the patterns to make ordered pairs. Graph the ordered pairs on this coordinate grid.

Subtract 3: 20

Subtract 2: 20

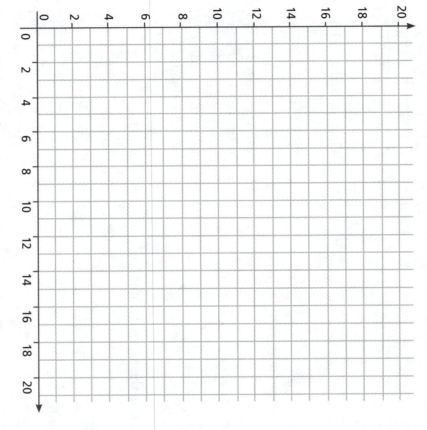

Describe the pattern shown by the points.

Answer: _____

Points Earned/Total = _____ /14

Mastery Test

Directions: Read each question and choose the best answer.

1 Evaluate this expression.

$$[(16 - 9) \times 2 - 10] \div 2$$

- Ⓐ 1
- Ⓑ 2
- Ⓒ 6
- Ⓓ 7

2 Which expression shows a number 8 times greater than 553 − 165?

- Ⓐ (553 − 165) × 8
- Ⓑ (553 − 165) ÷ 8
- Ⓒ (8 × 553) + 165
- Ⓓ 8 + (553 − 165)

3 Emma added 15 to 33 and then divided by the product of 2 times 2. Write the expression she used.

Answer: _____

4 Which expression can Ben evaluate to find the distance to the library and back if he drives 6 miles west and 4 miles south to get to the library?

- Ⓐ 2 + 6 + 4
- Ⓑ 2 × 6 + 4
- Ⓒ (6 + 4) × 2
- Ⓓ (6 × 2) × (4 × 2)

5 What is the value of the expression?

$$5 + \{2 + [15 - 3 \times (1 + 2)] + 3\}$$

- Ⓐ 10
- Ⓒ 24
- Ⓑ 16
- Ⓓ 46

6 Start at zero and write a sequence for each of these rules:

  Add 2

  Add 6

Describe the relationship between the corresponding terms in the two sequences.

Answer: _____

7 In the number 5,555 how many times greater is the 5 in the thousands place than the 5 in the hundreds place?

- Ⓐ 1 time
- Ⓑ 9 times
- Ⓒ 10 times
- Ⓓ 100 times

8 Which describes how to move the decimal point to divide by 0.01?

- Ⓐ Move the decimal point 1 place to the right.
- Ⓑ Move the decimal point 1 place to the left.
- Ⓒ Move the decimal point 2 places to the right.
- Ⓓ Move the decimal point 2 places to the left.

9 How much will 100 balloons cost if 1 balloon costs $1.09?

Answer: _____

GO ON

10 Matt bought 1,000 campaign buttons for $134.00. How much did each button cost?

Answer: _____

11 Write 100,000 in exponential notation.

Answer: _____

12 Write 10^3 in standard form.

Answer: _____

13 What is the standard form for $800,000 + 6,000 + 300 + 9 + 0.07$?

Ⓐ 860,309.7
Ⓑ 806,390.7
Ⓒ 86,309.07
Ⓓ 806,309.07

14 What is the place value of 1 in this number?

5,236.147

Ⓐ tens
Ⓑ tenths
Ⓒ hundredths
Ⓓ thousandths

15 Write 67.042 in word form.

Answer: _____

16 Which is *one hundred twenty-eight and seventy-nine hundredths* written as a decimal?

Ⓐ 128.79
Ⓑ 128.079
Ⓒ 100.2879
Ⓓ 100.79

17 Write >, =, or < to compare these decimals.

78.403 ☐ 78.043

Answer: _____

18 Shawnika ran on a treadmill for 5.78 miles. Round this distance to the nearest tenth of a mile.

Ⓐ 5.0 miles
Ⓑ 5.7 miles
Ⓒ 5.8 miles
Ⓓ 6.0 miles

19 $15 \times 2,345 =$

Ⓐ 13,060
Ⓑ 14,070
Ⓒ 34,175
Ⓓ 35,175

20 What is the value of b in the equation below?

$b \div 4 = 8$

Ⓐ 2
Ⓑ 4
Ⓒ 32
Ⓓ 40

21 Find the quotient.

$88\overline{)4,928}$

Ⓐ 45
Ⓑ 46
Ⓒ 56
Ⓓ 57

22 Ms. Castillo paid $6.87 for 3 pineapples. What was the cost of each pineapple?

ⓐ $2.29

ⓑ $3.87

ⓒ $20.61

ⓓ $22.80

23 Grapes cost $3.67 a pound. How much will 2.8 pounds of grapes cost? Round up to the nearest cent.

Answer: _____

24 The table shows prices of salads at a restaurant.

Garden	$2.35
Cheese and Tomato	$2.75
Mixed Veggie	$3.75
Fruit	$4.15
Chicken	$5.25
Shrimp	$5.85

Suki and her brother bought 2 mixed veggie salads. She gave the clerk $20 for both salads. How much change should she receive?

ⓐ $7.50

ⓑ $12.50

ⓒ $13.60

ⓓ $16.25

25 Irma bought two boxes of candy for Valentine's Day. The boxes weighed 2.3 pounds and 1.75 pounds. What was the total weight of the candy?

ⓐ 1.98 lb

ⓑ 3.05 lb

ⓒ 4.05 lb

ⓓ 4.15 lb

26 Guliana had 12.8 kilograms of potting soil. She used 6.25 kilograms to plant a bush. How many kilograms did she have left?

Answer: _____

27 A package of trail mix contains $\frac{5}{8}$ pound of nuts and $\frac{1}{4}$ pound of raisins. What is the total weight of the trail mix?

ⓐ $\frac{3}{8}$ pound

ⓑ $\frac{1}{2}$ pound

ⓒ $\frac{3}{4}$ pound

ⓓ $\frac{7}{8}$ pound

28 Kyle and Garrit are making model cars. Kyle's is $\frac{5}{6}$ foot long. Garrit's model is $\frac{1}{4}$ foot long. How much longer is Kyle's model?

ⓐ $\frac{2}{5}$ ft

ⓑ $\frac{1}{6}$ ft

ⓒ $\frac{7}{12}$ ft

ⓓ $1\frac{1}{12}$ ft

29 Tracy has $3\frac{3}{8}$ yards of fabric. She needs $5\frac{1}{8}$ yards of fabric to make a skirt. How much more fabric does Tracy need?

Ⓐ $1\frac{1}{4}$ yards

Ⓑ $1\frac{3}{4}$ yards

Ⓒ $2\frac{1}{4}$ yards

Ⓓ $2\frac{3}{4}$ yards

30 If 8 people divide 5 pies evenly, what fraction of a pie will each person get?

Ⓐ $\frac{1}{8}$

Ⓑ $\frac{3}{5}$

Ⓒ $\frac{5}{8}$

Ⓓ $1\frac{3}{5}$

31 If Gretchen divides 45 ounces of soup into 6 bowls, about how many ounces of soup will be in each bowl?

Ⓐ between 5 ounces and 6 ounces

Ⓑ between 6 ounces and 7 ounces

Ⓒ between 7 ounces and 8 ounces

Ⓓ between 8 ounces and 9 ounces

32 Julie needs to find $\frac{1}{3}$ of 36. Which describes how Julie can find the answer?

Ⓐ $\frac{1}{36} \times 3$

Ⓑ $36 \div 3$

Ⓒ 36×3

Ⓓ $\frac{1}{36} \div 3$

33 Use this area model to help you find the product $\frac{4}{7} \times \frac{2}{3}$.

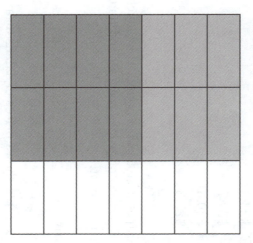

Answer: _____

34 Which statement describes the product of $5\frac{3}{4} \times \frac{3}{4}$?

Ⓐ The product is less than $5\frac{3}{4}$.

Ⓑ The product is greater than $5\frac{3}{4}$.

Ⓒ The product is less than $\frac{5}{6}$.

Ⓓ The product is 1.

35 Alex walked at $4\frac{1}{3}$ miles per hour for $1\frac{1}{2}$ hours. How far did he walk?

Ⓐ $2\frac{5}{6}$ miles

Ⓑ $5\frac{5}{6}$ miles

Ⓒ $6\frac{1}{2}$ miles

Ⓓ $8\frac{2}{3}$ miles

36 Elsa had $\frac{1}{3}$ of a cake left from her party. She divided it into 4 pieces. What fraction of the cake was each piece?

Answer: _____

37 How many $\frac{1}{8}$-pound bags of nuts can Jeremy make from 3 pounds of nuts?

Answer: _____

38 How many gallons are there in 12 quarts?

Ⓐ 3 gal
Ⓑ 6 gal
Ⓒ 24 gal
Ⓓ 48 gal

39 How many milliliters are there in 4 liters?

Ⓐ 0.004 mL   Ⓒ 400 mL
Ⓑ 0.04 mL   Ⓓ 4,000 mL

40 Kiram drove 4.3 kilometers to get to the store. How can he determine how many meters he drove?

Ⓐ divide by 100
Ⓑ divide by 1,000
Ⓒ multiply by 100
Ⓓ multiply by 1,000

41 Erin brought 3 gallons of fruit punch to a party. Each of the plastic glasses she brought can hold 1 pint. How many glasses can Erin fill?

Answer: _____

42 Each of the 15 students in a science class measured the amount of distilled water he or she made during an experiment. The line plot shows the results.

Volume of Distilled Water

$\frac{1}{8}$	$\frac{1}{4}$	$\frac{3}{8}$	$\frac{1}{2}$
X			X
X	X		X
X	X	X	X
X	X	X	X
X	X	X	X

Volume (in cups)

If the total amount of water is divided evenly among the 15 students, how much will each student get?

Answer: _____

43 What is the volume of this rectangular prism?

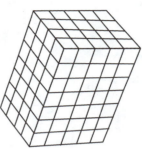

Ⓐ 68 cubic units
Ⓑ 83 cubic units
Ⓒ 120 cubic units
Ⓓ 140 cubic units

GO ON

44 How many cubic feet of dirt are needed to fill a hole that is 20 feet deep, 14 feet wide, and 10 feet long?

Ⓐ 280 ft³

Ⓑ 440 ft³

Ⓒ 2,800 ft³

Ⓓ 4,400 ft³

45 Dora has two storage boxes. One is an 18-inch-long, 18-inch-wide, 18-inch-tall cube. The other is 30 inches long, 20 inches wide, and 10 inches deep. What is the total volume of the two boxes?

Show all of your work. Explain in words the steps you follow. Write your answer on the answer line.

Answer: _____

Explanation: _____

_____

_____

_____

Tyler made this grid of his neighborhood and located his friends' homes. Use this coordinate grid for questions 46 and 47.

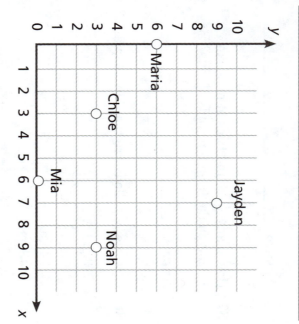

46 Who lives at (0, 6)?

Ⓐ Chloe

Ⓑ Jayden

Ⓒ Maria

Ⓓ Mia

47 What ordered pair shows the location of Noah's home?

Ⓐ (9, 3)

Ⓑ (9, 6)

Ⓒ (3, 9)

Ⓓ (6, 7)

48 Start at 0. Write sequences for the rules *Add 1* and *Add 3*. Use corresponding terms from the patterns to make ordered pairs. Graph the ordered pairs on this coordinate grid.

Add 1: 0, _____

Add 3: 0, _____

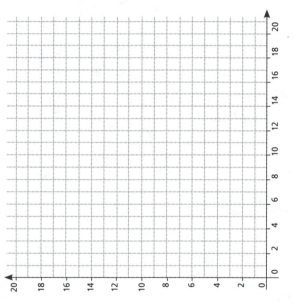

Describe the pattern shown by the points.

Answer: _____

49 Which statement is true?

Ⓐ All trapezoids are parallelograms.

Ⓑ All parallelograms are rectangles.

Ⓒ All rectangles are parallelograms.

Ⓓ The angles in a parallelogram are all acute.

50   Classify this quadrilateral.

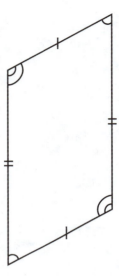

Ⓐ polygon, quadrilateral, parallelogram

Ⓑ quadrilateral, trapezoid, rhombus

Ⓒ parallelogram, rectangle, rhombus

Ⓓ parallelogram, rhombus, square

Points Earned/Total = _____ /50

STOP

Keeping Score

Common Core Math 5

	Points Earned / Total Points	Percent Score
Tryout Test	/50	%
Test Practice 1 Algebraic Thinking	/14	%
Test Practice 2 Number Sense	/20	%
Test Practice 3 Operations with Whole Numbers and Decimals	/18	%
Test Practice 4 Fractions	/16	%
Test Practice 5 Measurement and Data	/15	%
Test Practice 6 Geometry	/14	%
Mastery Test	/50	%

1. Fill in the number of points you earned in the Points Earned box.

2. Use the Finding Percent chart on page 104 to figure out your Percent Score. Then fill in the % box.

3. Compare your Percent Scores for the Tryout Test and the Mastery Test. See how much you've learned!

Finding Percent

Many tests give your score in both number of points earned and in percentages. This handy chart will tell you your percent score.

1. Find the band with the same number of points that are on your test.

2. Follow along the top row of the band to the number of points you earned. Your percent score is right below it.

Number of Questions on Test

14

1	2	3	4	5	6	7	8	9	10	11	12	13	14
7%	14%	21%	29%	36%	43%	50%	57%	64%	71%	79%	86%	93%	100%

15

1	2	3	4	5	6	7	8	9	10	11	12	13	14	15
7%	13%	20%	27%	33%	40%	47%	53%	60%	67%	73%	80%	87%	93%	100%

16

1	2	3	4	5	6	7	8	9	10	11	12	13	14	15	16
6%	13%	19%	25%	31%	38%	44%	50%	56%	63%	69%	75%	81%	88%	94%	100%

18

1	2	3	4	5	6	7	8	9	10	11	12	13	14	15	16	17	18
6%	11%	17%	22%	28%	33%	39%	44%	50%	56%	61%	67%	72%	78%	83%	89%	94%	100%

20

1	2	3	4	5	6	7	8	9	10	11	12	13	14	15	16
5%	10%	15%	20%	25%	30%	35%	40%	45%	50%	55%	60%	65%	70%	75%	80%

17	18	19	20
85%	90%	95%	100%

50

1	2	3	4	5	6	7	8	9	10	11	12	13	14	15	16	17	18
2%	4%	6%	8%	10%	12%	14%	16%	18%	20%	22%	24%	26%	28%	30%	32%	34%	36%

19	20	21	22	23	24	25	26	27	28	29	30	31	32	33	34	35	36
38%	40%	42%	44%	46%	48%	50%	52%	54%	56%	58%	60%	62%	64%	66%	68%	70%	72%

37	38	39	40	41	42	43	44	45	46	47	48	49	50
74%	76%	78%	80%	82%	84%	86%	88%	90%	92%	94%	96%	98%	100%